Agostino Ferran

The Month of Our Lady,

Under the Patronage of Our Blessed Lady of Victory

Agostino Ferran

The Month of Our Lady,
Under the Patronage of Our Blessed Lady of Victory

ISBN/EAN: 9783337105174

Printed in Europe, USA, Canada, Australia, Japan

Cover: Foto ©ninafisch / pixelio.de

More available books at **www.hansebooks.com**

NEW YORK, CINCINNATI, CHICAGO:

BENZIGER BROTHERS,

Printers to the Holy Apostolic See.

PREFACE.

DEVOTION to our Blessed Lady has been so long established among the faithful and is so universally known and practised, that any explanation on my part is unnecessary and superfluous. The compiler and translator has been induced to think that he would render a service to religion, and at the same time pay a tribute of devotion to the Mother of God, by presenting this old work in a new English dress.

That this little book may promote and foster among the faithful deep and heart-felt devotion to the Blessed Virgin Mary, is the prayer of

THE TRANSLATOR.

CONTENTS.

PAGE

MEDITATIONS

FOR THE

MONTH OF OUR LADY.

———

Mother of grace, O Mary blest!
To thee, sweet fount of love, we fly:
Shield us through life, and take us hence
To thy dear bosom when we die.

FIRST DAY.

WHY WE SHOULD PRACTISE DEVOTION TO THE BLESSED VIRGIN MARY.

"Her spirit is sweeter than honey, and her heritage than the honey-comb.   They that eat her shall yet be hungry, and they that drink her shall still thirst.   Whoso hearkeneth to her shall not be confounded, and they that work by her shall not sin."

AS a woman was instrumental in the fall of man, it was the will of God that a woman should co-operate in man's redemption.   During forty centuries the Lord, in the language of Isaias, observed attentively the illustrious women who from time to time appeared, in order to choose her who should be most worthy of himself and best adapted to the plan of the redemption of man.   Sara presented herself in the splendor of her wealth, Rebecca in the lustre of her beauty, and Rachel in the elegance of her grace; but their wealth, beauty, and grace had no attractions for the Most High. Ruth, Jahel and Judith, Abigail and Es-

ther, appeared in succession; but none
of these was chosen. They were all figures of that exalted maiden in whom the
virtues and worth of each and all of them
were to be united. Who then will be
that illustrious woman foretold by the
prophets, longed for by the patriarchs,
foreshown from the earliest days in symbols and figures so numerous and so various, and promised by the Almighty from
the beginning? Lovely daughter of
Joachim and Anne, thou art the chosen
one! Although many maidens have arrayed themselves in garments of glory,
Mary far surpasses them in abundance of
merit and fulness and richness of reward.
Mary, as well in the order of nature as in
the order of grace and glory, far excels
all women, all just souls, and even all
angelic beings united; for she alone attracted the especial preference of Almighty God, and was selected by him to
be the mother of his Son, and thus to co-
operate in our redemption. Wishing to
consecrate to the honor of Our Lady the
month of May, we shall commence our
exercises of piety by considering the
principal motives which urge us, as
Christians, to pay to her the tribute of
our devotion. The first is because
amongst all created beings she is adorned

with transcendent sanctity, the second because she is the mother of God and also our mother.

I.

It being our duty to love God principally because he contains essentially in himself every perfection, and it being likewise our duty to praise God in his saints, it becomes our duty to be especially devoted to Mary; because amongst all the creatures of God she is the most pure, the most holy, the most perfect. As such we discover her in the designs of the Lord; and the church of God's infallible truth applies to this great mother in a mystic sense whatever the Scripture says of the divine Wisdom. Hence Mary is made to say of herself:—I came out of the mouth of the Most High, the first born before all creatures (*Eccl.* xxiv. 5). The Lord possessed me in the beginning of his ways, before he made anything from the beginning. I was set up from eternity, and of old before the earth was made. The depths were not as yet, and I was already conceived; neither had the fountains of water as yet sprung out... When he prepared the heavens, I was present;

when with a certain law and compass he enclosed the depths, I was with him forming all things (*Prov.* viii. 22). I was exalted like a cedar in Libanus, and as a cypress tree on Mount Sion. I was exalted like a palm tree in Cades, and as a rose plant in Jericho (*Eccl.* xxiv. 17).

Mary is thus celebrated by the spouse of the Canticles : Thou art all fair, O my love ; and there is not a spot in thee. Thou comest forth as the morning rising, fair as the moon, bright as the sun (*Cant.* iv. 7). It is not surprising, therefore, that the angel of God, when in the fulness of time he visited Mary as a messenger from the Most High, exclaimed on beholding her,—Hail, full of grace ; the Lord is with thee : blessed art thou among women (*Luke* i. 28).

In like manner, the Fathers of the Church proclaimed Mary the most holy and most lovely creature that ever issued from the hands of Him that is mighty. The eternal God, says St. Bernardine, created in time his holy mother, such as he had chosen her from eternity, adorning her with all the gifts of nature and grace, which became the grandeur of his majesty. With the exception of Christ, and with the exception also of his most blessed mother, says

St. Cyril, we were all born in sin. Mary was an object of wonder to angels and to men, says Albertus Magnus, because all that human nature, all that a mere creature is capable of being endowed with, was found in Mary. What is more holy, says St. Thomas, than Mary? Neither Prophets, nor Apostles, nor Martyrs, nor Patriarchs, nor Thrones, nor Dominations, nor Cherubim, nor Seraphim. Amongst all created beings, visible and invisible, nothing greater or more excellent than she can be found. According to Suarez, Mary surpasses in sanctity, not only every saint and every angel individually considered, but all saints and all angels united. Mary, therefore, is, in the words of the Church, Queen of all saints, because in holiness and perfection she far excels them.

II.

If we owe honor to Mary as the most holy of all creatures, what honor do we not owe to her as the mother of God? Behold, a virgin shall conceive, and bear a son, says Isaias (vii. 14). This virgin is Mary, this son of Mary is the Son of

God. The angel Gabriel sent from God, said : Fear not, Mary; for thou hast found grace with God.   Behold, thou shalt conceive in thy womb, and shalt bring forth a son ; and thou shalt call his name Jesus. He shall be great, and shall be called the son of the Most High (*Luke* iv. 30).

In the motherhood of the Holy Virgin are founded her glories ; and the Church delights to address her by all those titles which correspond to so great a dignity. Nothing can be of so great honor to the creature as to be the mother of the Creator.` To have given to the light of the world the divine wisdom, that was from the beginning with God, and in the beginning was God; by whom all things were made, and without whom was made nothing that was made (*John* i), is undoubtedly the loftiest dignity that the mind is capable of conceiving in a mere creature. The blessed Virgin may be considered as the gate and dwelling place of the divine wisdom that cries aloud:— Blessed is the man that heareth me, and that watcheth daily at my gate, and waiteth at the posts of my doors(*Prov.* viii. 34). She is the gate of wisdom, because through her, and with a body taken from her, the Son of God entered into the world for our salvation. She is the dwelling place of wisdom; because the divine wisdom, that is discovered in others by a communication of light, is found in Mary in an especial manner by the abode which God made man took up in her bosom. We may therefore approach the divine wisdom by the same way in which he condescended to come to us. We may also learn how to receive the precepts and observe the counsels of divine wisdom from the example of her who kept all these things in her heart, and to whom the holy Elizabeth said, by inspiration of the spirit of God,—Blessed art thou that hast believed; because those things shall be accomplished that were spoken to thee by the Lord (*Luke* i. 45).

It was the intention of Almighty God that Mary, in becoming the mother of Christ, should become also our mother. And this is the third title by which she challenges our respect and honor. Mary, says William the Abbot, has one only Son; still she is the mother of many. By being mother of the head, she is the mother of many members.   Hence she is called Mother of all Christians, and receives from them the honor which is due to such a mother.   Mary is our mother, because she has restored to us the life of grace, of which we were deprived by our first mother. As Eve, says Richard of St. Lawrence, was called the mother of the living, from the natural life which she gave to men, with greater reason is Mary called the mother of all the living, from the life of grace which men receive only through her agency. Mary is, moreover, our mother, because she is the mother of the Son of God, who deigned to call us his brothers. Let us all then rejoice, says St. Bonaventure; let us all cry aloud with exultation:—Blessed be the Brother through whom Mary is our mother; and blessed be the mother through whom Christ is our brother. Mary is our mother because she was given to us as a mother by our divine Redeemer, and adopted us as her children in the person of St. John. When Jesus, agonizing on the cross, saw his mother and the disciple standing, whom he loved, he saith to his mother: Woman, behold thy son. After that he saith to his disciple: Behold thy mother. And from that hour the disciple took her to his own (*John* xix. 21). From what has been said, we cannot but conclude that we are bound to love and honor Mary in an especial manner, both because she is the most pure and holy of all creatures, and because, whilst she is truly the mother of God made man, she is also our own most loving mother.

ASPIRATION.

Holy Mary, mother of God, pray for us sinners.

PRACTICE.

Be careful to utter no word that may be displeasing to your heavenly Mother.

LITANY.

Read a chapter of the Glories of Mary.

SECOND DAY.

HOW WE SHOULD HONOR THE BLESSED VIRGIN MARY.

" Thou art the glory of Jerusalem; thou art the joy of Israel; thou art the honor of our people." *Judith* xv. 10.

JUDITH, having returned from the Assyrian camp, presented herself to the people of Bethulia and thus addressed them: Praise ye the Lord, our God, who hath not forsaken them that hope in him. And by me, his handmaid, he hath fulfilled his mercy, which he promised to the house of Israel: and he hath killed the enemy of his people by my hand this night (*Judith* xiii. 17, 18).

Who does not perceive in Judith victorious over Holofernes our great mother Mary, through whom the world was delivered from the slavery of sin? In the public homage paid to Judith by the people of Bethulia, who does not discover the homage which by Christians should be paid to Mary? The Church, revering her as the most lovely, the most holy, and most noble of all mere creatures, acknowledging her as the mother of God and the mother of all Christians, pronounces separation from the true fold against any one who should attempt to detract from the honor due to her, and to tarnish her glory (Council of Ephesus). Having considered the principal motives which should influence us to be devout to Mary, let us now consider in what manner we ought to love her ; and convince ourselves that the honor which we should tribute to Mary consists in the first place *in the feelings of the heart;* and in the second, in the *external manifestation of these feelings.*

I.

The true worship of God commences in the understanding, and is completed

in the heart. It is the part of the
understanding to make us know and admire him, and of the heart to love and
obey him; so that, from a just knowledge
of God, true love for him flows. From
this principle it follows, that devotion to
the great mother of God must be established in the heart in order to prove sincere and advantageous. Almighty God
says: "My son, give me thy heart" (*Prov.*
xxv. 26), showing that he requires us to
love him with the heart, and that he desires nothing so much as the offering of
the heart. Hence, to be truly devout to
Mary, we must be devout to her with the
whole heart. Among the principal affections of the heart are three: Love,
sympathetic pleasure, and reverence.
The affection of love is a feeling of
the soul turned towards an object that
attracts us. It has its origin in the esteem in which we hold the object and the
worth which we discover in it. Who
then will refuse to love Mary? Was not
she alone, amongst all creatures, unsullied by sin in her conception? And did
she not pass her whole life without blemish in the sight of God? Is she not the
mother of God, and, as his mother, enthroned in Heaven Queen of Saints and of
Angels? And does she not, with a

mother's heart, earnestly desire the happiness of all her children on earth ? Who, therefore, can withhold from Mary the warmest and most tender feeling of the soul : deep, unfeigned, heartfelt love ?

To find pleasure in the grace and favors bestowed upon Mary, belongs to the affection of sympathetic pleasure. To reflect that Mary was chosen by God, and elevated to the most sublime dignity of being his mother ; that she was adorned with the most exalted graces, and enriched with the rarest gifts ; that in Heaven her glory is. inferior to that only of the Father, Son, and Holy Ghost; that for forty centuries the Prophets of the Lord had their eyes fixed upon her and foreshowed her by symbols and figures without number ; that she was the desire of the Patriarchs and of the souls of all the just deceased before Christ ;— to reflect upon all this, and to experience delight in the reflection, is to honor Mary and to furnish a great proof of love. Thus a friend rejoices in the welfare and prosperity of a friend.

This homage of sympathetic pleasure gives honor to the Blessed Virgin, and is so pleasing to her that she invites us with the Church to rejoice with her, because she pleased the Most High, and at the appointed time became the mother of God made man. For this reason both the Church militant and the Church triumphant feel great complacency in the dignity and glory of Mary. St. Bonaventure exclaims: O Holy Virgin, in whose glory all the choirs of Saints exult and rejoice! The Church chants with jubilation—Let us all rejoice, celebrating a festive day in honor of the Blessed Virgin Mary, whose assumption is a source of joy to the Angels of God. On this day the Blessed Virgin ascended to Heaven : rejoice, because with Christ she reigns forever.

But of what value would be our love for Mary and our rejoicing with her, if to love and pleasure we did not add the feeling of reverence ? The degree of reverence, of humble respect due to a person, is determined by that person's exaltation, dignity and greatness. Was not Mary saluted by an Angel as full of grace, and as having the Lord with her (*Luke* i. 28) ? Was it not announced to her that she was to become the mother of the Most High, without blemish to her virginal purity ? Did not God become in some measure dependent on Mary, by becoming her Son? He was subject to them (to Mary and Joseph), says St. Luke.

Mary, by being made the mother of God, became our mother and the Queen of Heaven and Earth. The mother of the Lord is the most dignified of all mothers. A greater than she is, God himself cannot form. A greater world than this world of ours, greater heavens, God can make; but a greater mother than the mother of God, God himself cannot produce. And why? Because, according to St. Thomas Aquinas, Mary, by becoming the mother of God, approached the confines of Divinity, and by being the mother of Him who alone is omnipotent and infinite, she also acquired a kind of infinity. Mary, says Peter Damian, is so perfect a work, that there is naught above her but God himself. Let every creature be silent and tremble, says the same St. Peter, and let no one dare to lift his eyes to the immensity of so great dignity,—So great, subjoins St. Bernard, that only God can comprehend it. We must therefore conclude that it is our duty to reverence Mary with the most profound sentiments of respect and veneration.

II.

Although God alone is in himself deserving of our invocations and our prayers, and him alone we acknowledge as the bestower of every good gift, and the fountain from which every blessing flows, still the very love which we cherish for God obliges us to have recourse to Mary by prayer and invocation. The Scriptures teach us that it is our interest to invoke the aid of the Saints who are reigning in heaven with Christ. We learn from the prophet Zacharias that the Angel of the Lord prayed for Jerusalem and the cities of Juda (*Zach.* i. 12) ; from the second book of Machabees (xv. 14), that Onias and Jeremias after their death prayed much for the people and for all the holy city ; in the Apocalypse (v. 8), the four and twenty ancients offer to the Lamb the prayers of the Saints. When impious men, such as Eunomius, Vigilantius, the Iconoclasts, and others, attempted to disturb the peace of the Christian family by refusing to the Saints the honors which belong to them, the Fathers by their writings and discourses, and the Church by her anathemas, assembled and condemned the sin of heresy. May the martyrs pray for us, says the Council of Chalcedon. Let us do all things in the fear of God, expecting also the intercession of our spotless Lady, the Holy Virgin Mary, and of the holy Angels, and of all the Saints.

These are the sentiments of the second Council of Nice and of the Council of Ephesus: No one, exclaims St. Germanus, obtains salvation unless through thee, O most holy Virgin! No one is delivered from evil unless through thy intercession, O purest of the pure! To no one is imparted a gift of grace, unless through thy mediation, O most chaste of the daughters of Eve! Who then can hesitate to invoke the most holy name of Mary? Who will not join in the salutation of the angel: Hail, full of grace? Who will not say to her with deepest veneration: Holy Mary, Mother of God? Who will not address her in the words of the Church of truth: Hail, holy Queen, Mother of Mercy? He who, says a Saint, apostrophizing Mary, he who shall assert of thee, O Holy Virgin, every thing that is illustrious and glorious, will never depart from the truth; and yet, language will not be able to express the greatness of thy dignity. We may then affirm with St. Germanus that, as *respiration* is a certain sign of bodily life, so the assiduous invocation of the sacred name of the Blessed Virgin is not only a sign of spiritual life, but a sure means of procuring choicest spiritual favors. It is our interest, therefore, to invoke the name and implore the assistance of Mary ; and sincere love for her should cause us to send forth our supplications from a heart throbbing with feelings of reverence, pleasure, complacency, praise, and gratitude.

ASPIRATION.

Teach me to praise thee, most Holy Virgin.

PRACTICE.

Endeavor to excite devotion to Mary in the hearts of others.

LITANY.

Read a chapter of Father Faber's Foot of the Cross.

THIRD DAY.

HOW WE SHOULD IMITATE THE BLESSED VIRGIN MARY.

"She is the unspotted Mirror of God's Majesty, and the image of his goodness." *Wisd.* vii. 26.

AMONGST the mystic titles which the Church applies to Mary, she calls her the *Mirror of Justice ;* that is, according to the Fathers, the Mirror of all virtues. God, and none but God, is the Sun of

Justice (*Malach.* iv. 2) ; but since Mary is adorned with gifts of grace far more abundantly than all other creatures, and since the reflection of her virtues reaches us, we very appropriately style her Mirror of Justice. God, says St. Thomas, formed a mirror, of all mirrors the brightest, the purity of which is so great that in vain would we seek one more pure without mounting to God himself. This Mirror is the most glorious Virgin whom, according to St. Bernard, God made the lively image of his own goodness. Let us then direct our view to this Mirror, and behold in it how we ought to practise obedience, humility and purity. All will see in it the example of Mary teaching them the life of holiness that will render secure the attainment of eternal bliss. Let us now consider that the interior honor which we owe to Mary, must seek its perfection in the imitation of her virtues and the avoidance of sin.

I.

Our Divine Redeemer says in the Gospel of St. Matthew (vii. 15. 21): Beware of false prophets, who come to you in the clothing of sheep, but inwardly they are ravenous wolves. By their fruits you shall know them. Do men gather grapes of thorns, or figs of thistles? Even so every good tree yieldeth good fruit, and the bad tree yieldeth bad fruit. A good tree cannot yield bad fruit; neither can a bad tree yield good fruit. Wherefore by their fruits you shall know them. Not every one that saith to me, Lord, Lord, shall enter into the kingdom of heaven : but he that doeth the will of my Father, who is in heaven, he shall enter into the kingdom of heaven. This language of Christ attentively considered, shows us clearly what we should do. These works have their source in the heart and we are taught that since we are bound to love God with our whole heart, we must manifest this love by the purity of our actions.

In like manner, the love which Mary's merits demand of us, can never be true and sincere, unless our faith in her is shown by our good deeds. Without these our devotion would be vain and illusory. Faith, says the Apostle St. James, faith without works is dead. No homage therefore is so worthy of the Saints as the imitation of their virtues. If we wish to enjoy the society of the Saints, says St. Augustine, let us imitate them; for that we may be certain of their intercession in our behalf, it is necessary that they recognize in us something of their own virtues. If we wish, consequently, our souls to be animated with genuine piety towards the most pure Virgin; if we wish to experience her patronage in all our necessities; if we wish to enjoy her company in the region of the Blessed, we must apply ourselves to the study of her virtues, and exert ourselves to form our life in imitation of hers. It is well to reserve our heart for Mary, and to direct towards her our affections; it is well to rejoice in the favors which she has received and in the dignity to which she has been elevated; it is well to bow with reverence before her and invoke assiduously her illustrious name; but unless we employ ourselves in the imitation of her virtues, fruitless will be our devotion. To praise Mary, says St. Augustine, without striving to imitate her example, would be nothing but the merest adulation.

The Holy Virgin is the most pure mirror of all virtues: in her we can discover what we ought to avoid, and what we ought to pursue. "Mary," says St. Gregory, "is the support of believers, the perfect example of pious souls." "Such was Mary," says St. Ambrose, "that her life is a rule for all Christians; from her all may learn what they should correct, what they should avoid, what they should perform. The Divine Spouse finds far greater pleasure in devout imitation, than in idle praise : and indeed the true praise of the heart is the imitation of the example." St. Jerome says: "Love Mary whom you honor, honor Mary whom you love. Then you truly honor and love her, if you study to imitate her life of love." From her lips the Church causes to issue the words of the divine wisdom. "Now therefore, ye children, hear me : Blessed are they that keep my ways. Hear instruction, and be wise, and refuse it not. Blessed is the man that heareth me, and that watcheth daily at my gates, and waiteth at the posts of my doors. He that findeth me shall find life, and shall have salvation from the Lord" (*Wisd.* viii. 32-35).

We must now consider how and when especially we ought to imitate Mary. If you are assaulted by a temptation against purity, lift your eyes to the image of Mary, and the thought cannot fail to recur to you that the Virgin of Virgins held virginity in such esteem, that she would have renounced the dignity of Mother of God offered to her by the messenger of the Lord, rather than consent to any blemish of her virginal purity. If you are assailed by discouragement, in adversity, turn to the image of Mary, and recalling to mind that this great Queen of Martyrs stood, with perfect resignation and submission to the will of God, at the foot of the cross, on which her only Son was dying in agony, you must feel encouraged to imitate her example. If you are tempted against faith or grow weak in the midst of the persecutions and disappointments of this life, lift your eyes to the image of Mary, and you will gain vigor from the reflection that this Queen of Apostles, by her presence, her word, and her admirable life, animated the Apostles and first believers in Christ, whilst for fidelity to Him they were subjected without intermission to every species of persecution. Whatever may be your trials, whencesoever may arise the agitation of your soul, look at the image of Mary, and learn from her the virtues that will strengthen you in trial, that will soothe into order and calmness the troubled waters of your spirit. Thus will you practise the imitation of Mary.

Mary is very properly called a mirror without spot; because, as by means of the mirror the blemishes of the countenance and the disorder of the garments are discovered and removed, so, by observing attentively the Holy Virgin, we learn how to frame our conduct and regulate all the actions of life. The Redeemer said to those Jews that believed in him : If you continue in my word, you shall be my disciples indeed (*John* viii. 31). If you be the children of Abraham, do the works of Abraham (viii. 39). We therefore being children of Mary, should imitate her chastity, her generosity, her humility, her benignity, her meekness, and her mercy. By so doing we shall secure for ourselves a rich reward, since Mary says to those who imitate her: He that shall find me shall find life, and shall have salvation from the Lord (*Prov.* viii. 35). That is, he who hearkens to Mary and imitates her example shall have bestowed upon him in this life treasures of graces, and in the life to come immortal glory.

II.

Most pleasing to Mary is the study of her devout servants to imitate her virtues, and she derives honor from their zealous exertions ; but one homage she demands of them with especial earnestness—an unceasing anxiety to shun sin. O, how great an evil is mortal sin ! It is the only true evil ; it is sovereign evil, unmingled, absolute evil. In committing mortal sin, a covenant is made with hell (*Is.* xxviii. 15); the spirit of Satan against God is shared in ; God is disobeyed, is despised, is rebelled against, is insulted ; and Christ is crucified anew. By sin the commandments of Christ are treated with scorn ; his blood is trampled under foot ; his favors, his merits, his graces, his rewards, all the blessings of God, are contemptuously cast away, and men think unjustly, in their folly, that God shall be like to themselves (*Ps.* xix. 20). The sinner forfeits eternal salvation, sacrifices to his passions endless happiness, draws down upon himself the thunderbolts of God's anger, and closes his earthly career by rushing headlong into the flames of everlasting perdition. If to God the wicked and his wickedness are hateful alike (*Wisd.* xiv. 9), it follows that Mary must detest sin, and that she can never grant her protection to those who are hateful to God and declared enemies of her Son.

If we wish, therefore, to do honor to Mary, we must be assiduous in our anxiety to avoid sin. It is our duty to give praise to Mary; but since praise is not seemly in the mouth of a sinner (*Eccl.* xv. 9), nor acceptable to the Almighty, in such praise Mary can never find complacency. We should love Mary in sincerity of heart; but if the heart is made the dwelling place of sin and sinful affections, how can our love for Mary be sincere? Mary is the Mother of God, the Queen of heaven and earth, the Treasurer of all heavenly graces, the Advocate of sinners. We must, therefore, if we value the favor of Heaven, offer to her our supplications and our prayers. But, he that turneth away his ears from hearing the law, his prayer shall be an abomination (*Prov.* xxviii.9),therefore, that our prayers may meet with favor in the sight of Mary, they must proceed from a repentant heart, at the command of a will firmly resolved to preserve itself free from every sin.

Devotion to Mary, to be true, must be profound and fruitful, deep-seated in the heart, and proving the uprightness of the will by works. Mary, in the words of Ecclesiasticus mystically applied to her by the Church, says : The Creator of all things commanded and said to me; and he that made me rested in my tabernacle, and he said to me: Let thy dwelling be in Jacob, and thy inheritance in Israel, and take root in my elect (*Eccl.* xxiv.12.14). And I took root in an honorable people, and in the portion of my God, his inheritance: and my abode is in the full assembly of saints (xxiv. 16). True devotion, therefore, must have its roots in the heart and not dwell merely upon the lips. Many ask of God and receive not because they ask amiss (*James* iv. 3). Like the Jews, they draw near to the Lord, and with their lips glorify him; but their heart is far from him (*Is.* xxix. 13). In like manner, many content themselves with reciting, in a hurried manner, the Rosary, or other prayers in honor of the Blessed Virgin, or with a careless visit to her image on festival days; but they never think of consecrating to her the throbbings of the heart, far more precious in her eyes than all mere bodily homage. Man seeth those things that appear, but the Lord beholdeth the heart (1 *Kings* xvi. 7); and into the inmost recesses of the heart Mary wishes to penetrate, to cast root downward, and bear fruit upward (*Is.* xxvii. 31).

ASPIRATION.

Holy mother, obtain for me purity of life.

PRACTICE.

Perform some acts of solid virtue in honor of Mary.

LITANY.

Read Mary Queen of May, by Brother Azarias.

FOURTH DAY.

HOW WE SHOULD HONOR THE MOST HOLY NAME OF MARY.

"The Lord called thy name a great olive tree, fair, fruitful, and beautiful."—*Jer.* xi. 16.

GOD hath exalted his Son, and hath given him a name which is above every name; that in the name of Jesus every knee should bow, of those who are in heaven, on earth, and in hell; and that every tongue should confess that the Lord Jesus Christ is in the glory of God the Father (*Phil.* ii. 9). To Mary, also, says Richard of St. Lawrence, the most holy Trinity has given a name that is above every name after that of her Son, and has endowed it with so great majesty and power, that all the creatures of heaven, earth, and hell bow with reverence when they hear it pronounced. Blessed be the Lord because he has so exalted the name of Mary that her praise shall never cease amongst the children of men. From the treasures of the Divinity the name of Mary is drawn, and it is so august in glory and power that its mysterious significations can never be fully explained. A shadow of this name was presented by the prophet Jeremias under the symbol of an olive tree, fair, fruitful, and beautiful. The glory and majesty of Mary were likened by Ecclesiasticus to a fair olive tree in the plains. And the spouse of the Canticles expressed its virtue under the figure of oil. Thy name is as oil poured out (*Cant.* i. 2). The signification of the name of Mary shows that it is a name of glory, expressing her most peculiar prerogatives of excellence; and it is also a name of the highest utility to men. As a name of glory we should frequently repeat it. As a name of utility, we should frequently invoke it, both in life and in death.

I.

The Church commemorates, with annual solemnity, the heroic virtues and noble achievements of the saints. Every year also she not only commemorates the different virtues and triumphs of Mary but assigns a day to be especially consecrated to the honor of her most sacred name. To this distinction the Virgin of Nazareth has a rightful claim ; because, according to the Fathers, her name issued from the treasures of the Divinity, and was imposed upon her by her parents, in obedience to a revelation made to them by an angel of the Lord. Names imposed by the Almighty, says St. Thomas, signify the grace imparted to those to whom such names are given. The name of Mary, according to St. Ambrose, signifies Mother of God. And indeed, the Holy Virgin was designated in the eternal decrees as the first-born of creatures, only because she was to be the temple of the living God, and the mother of the eternal Word made flesh.

St. Bernardine reasons as follows: As the Son of God sits at the right hand of the Father on high, being made so much better than the angels, as he has inherited a more excellent name above them, which name implies that he is the Son of God, of the same nature with his Father, so also the Virgin Mary, mother of our Lord Jesus Christ, has been made so much better than the angels as she has inherited a more excellent name above all pure creatures—the name of Mother of God. No other creature, says St. Bonaventure, can appropriately bear this illustrious name. The dignity of Mary is announced by her name, says St.

Chrysologus, Mary, that is, sovereign lady. Mary, adds St. Bonaventure, "is sovereign mistress of the angels in heaven, of the men on earth, and the demons in hell." As soon as Mary was destined to be the mother of the Lord she received a kind of supreme authority, inherent in this title, in this imcomparable dignity; just as, amongst men, the spouse of him who is elevated to distinguished power, assuming the title of the family, his state, condition, and name. Hence the Blessed Virgin at her birth received the name of Mary in view of that which she was to become, and of the dignity to which God had predestined her. If Christ, then, is the Lord and Ruler of the universe, Mary has been appointed the sovereign mistress of all creatures, and whoever bends the knee to Jesus should bow suppliantly in the presence of his mother Mary.

The name of Mary, moreover, is a name of most happy augury for him who shows it honor; for it signifies also star of the sea. Hail, Star of the Sea, is a salutation addressed to Mary by the Church. The Holy Virgin, says St. Ambrose, is the polar star that guides safely to the harbor of salvation. The world may be likened to a tempest-tossed ocean, filled with rocks and shoals, and monsters. How shall we escape destruction in navigating it? Our only hope is to have recourse to Mary, our guiding-star. By following her we shall reach the port uninjured. Mary, says St. Thomas, is called a Star; and as mariners reach the haven under the guidance of the stars, Christians reach glory conducted by Mary.

According to the Fathers of the Church, the name of Mary is also interpreted Sea, because, as the Sea is the receptacle of all the waters of the earth, Mary is the receptacle of all graces. The angel saluted her, Hail, full of grace (*Luke* i. 28), St. John Damascene calls her an abyss of grace. Hence, concludes blessed Denis, as no one can number the drops of water in the ocean, no one can express the abundance of the grace and the greatness of the glory of Mary.

St. Thomas and St. Bonaventure interpret the name of Mary, Enlightened and Enlightening; for she is the mother of Him who is the true light of the world, and approaching more nearly than any other creature the Sun of Justice—light by essence. None other has received light so abundantly, and none is so well prepared to communicate it to others. She is the dawn that ushered in Him who enlighteneth every man that cometh into this world (*John* i. 9). Nations enlightened by Jesus Christ, people sitting before in darkness and in the shadow of death (*Luke* i. 79), you have seen a great light. But by means of whom ? By means of Mary, who gave to the world the Sun of Justice. She is the great wonder that appeared in heaven to St. John—a woman clothed with the sun, and the moon under her feet, and on her head a crown of twelve stars (*Apoc.* xii. 1). She with her light enlightened the world, but she herself was irradiated by infinite light, and in virtue of her name was enlightened and enlightener. Let then the glorious name of Mary, telling of her grandeur, be re-echoed with hope and trust, joy and triumph, by all her children.

II.

The name of Mary is, besides, replete with grace and benedictions, and can never be uttered without advantage to him who devoutly invokes it. According to St. Ambrose, the name of Mary is a sweet ointment that breathes the odor of divine grace. It has been compared in its virtue to oil, for it heals the sick, diffuses around a delicious odor, and enkindles in the heart the fire of divine love. So great is the virtue of the name of Mary, that devoutly invoked, it softens the hardness of the sinner's heart, and encourages him to hope for pardon for the past, and for grace to lead a virtuous life. The name of Mary is a tower of strength; if the sinner flies to her for succor, all tenderness and compassion as she is, he shall assuredly obtain salvation. No infirmity is so malignant that it will not yield without delay to the efficacy of her name (*St. Ambrose*). Take courage then, O sinners; if your sins be as scarlet, they shall, through the intercession of Mary, be made as white as snow; and if they be red as crimson, they shall be white as wool (*Is.* i. 18). The invocation of the name of Mary, says the pious à Kempis, is a short prayer, easy to be remembered, sweet to be thought of, and powerful to protect us against all our enemies.

Every one knows, from sad experience, how his soul is harassed by the rebellion of passion and the assaults of temptation. But Mary is our shield in youth and in old age, in life and in death. The spirits of darkness, says à Kempis, dread the name of Mary, and when they hear it invoked, they flee as from consuming

flames (*L.* iv. *ad. Novit*). Not more rap-
idly, adds St. Bonaventure, is wax melted
before the fire, than the demons turn in
precipitate flight at the sound of the
most holy name of Mary (*in Spec.*).
Satan assails us with all the fury of temptation in the last hour of life, but the devout invocation of the name of Mary
dissipates every fear (*St. Bon. Spec.*).
Hence we may affirm again with St. Germanus, that as respiration is a certain sign
of life in the body, so the frequent invocation of the name of Mary is either a sure
sign of the life of grace, or that grace
will soon be obtained. For she has
power, says Gerson, to accomplish the
reconciliation of the sinner with God, to
open the gates of heaven, to give
strength to us against all the power of the
air, and to render assistance in every
necessity of soul and body. The name of
Mary therefore expresses her greatness,
and is beneficial to those who devoutly
invoke it, in life and in death.

ASPIRATION.

Hail, Queen of Heaven ! Queen of Angels !

PRACTICE.

Invoke frequently the name of Mary, a

name of joy to angels, of usefulness to men, and of terror to demons.

LITANY.

Read Father Faber's Hymns.

FIFTH DAY.

HOW WE SHOULD HONOR MARY AS MOTHER OF GOD.

"There shall come forth a rod out of the root of Jesse, and a flower shall rise up out of his root." *Is.* xi. i.

WHILST the Jews were becoming every day more deeply immersed in iniquity, and when Jerusalem had renounced the covenant of the Lord by idolatry and depravity of morals, the prophet Isaias arose, who foretold to the people of Juda their future captivity in Babylon and their subsequent liberation. These prophecies, as sacred commentators understand them, symbolized other events far more sublime and important : the slavery of the human race under the power of Satan, and its future liberation by Jesus Christ. And the prophet, indeed, with his mind filled with the spirit of God, and eyes fixed on the ages to come, exclaimed : There shall come forth a rod from the root of Jesse, and a flower shall rise up out of his root. And the spirit of wisdom and of understanding, the spirit of the Lord shall rest upon him, the spirit of counsel and of fortitude, the spirit of knowledge and of godliness (*Is.* xi. 12). But the mystic rod and the prophetic flower, what do they signify? The Fathers of the Church with one voice reply, the rod is Mary, the flower is Jesus Christ, her Son. Isaias himself had already declared to Achaz: Behold, a virgin shall conceive, and shall bear a son ; and his name shall be called Emmanuel (*Is.* vii. 14). Mary therefore, under the obscurity of symbols and figures, was prophetically pointed out to the people of the Lord before the coming of our divine Redeemer; and we, who live under the peaceful empire of the law of grace, hold as a dogma of our religious faith, that Mary is the true mother of God. And as from her motherhood arise all the greatness, the gifts, and the privileges of Mary, and all the good that descends to us through her, we owe to Mary especial honor : first, because she is the mother of **God ;** secondly, because she **enjoys the** greatest dignity that can be bestowed on a mere human creature.

I.

The oracles of the prophets had ceased, and the sceptre had been taken away from Juda (*Gen.* xlix. 10). Just souls had begun to discern the termination of their sighs in the completion of the seventy weeks predicted by Daniel (*Dan.* xi. 25); with Mary had appeared the dawn which announced the approaching rising of the Sun of Justice : then the angel Gabriel descends from the highest heavens, and presents himself before the youthful Virgin Mary, and says to her: Hail, full of grace, the Lord is with thee: blessed art thou among women. Fear not, Mary, for thou hast found grace with God: behold, thou shalt conceive, and bring forth a son; and thou shalt call his name Jesus. He shall be great, and shall be called the Son of the Most High: and the Lord God shall give unto him the throne of David his father; and he shall reign in the house of Jacob forever (*Luke* i. 28-32). Mary, however, being a virgin, and having consecrated herself to God from her earliest years, and wishing to preserve unsullied her virginal purity, said to the angel: How shall this be done, because I know not man? And the angel answering, said to her: The Holy Ghost shall come upon thee, and the power of the Most High shall overshadow thee, and therefore also the Holy One who shall be born of thee shall be called the Son of God (*Luke* i. 34, 35).

Heaven and earth awaited with anxiety the answer of Mary; for in the eternal decress of God, her consent was one of the requisite conditions of the incarnation. The souls of the departed just prayed for the consent of the Virgin, that heaven might be opened to their entrance. The angel was anxious to bear a speedy answer to the Father from whom he had received his mission. The Son of God waited only to hear her speak,—Be it done to me according to thy word,—to descend from heaven and unite in her bosom the divine with the human nature. Return, O Mary! cries out St. Bernard, the reply wished for by heaven and earth. The sovereign Lord of all things, who desires thy comeliness, now desires thy consent, on which depends the salvation of the world. And him, to whom thou wast pleasing in silence, thou wilt please still more by speaking.

Mary became the mother of God. Rising up she went into the mountainous country with haste, into a city of Juda; and she entered into the house of Zachary and saluted Elizabeth. And it came to pass when Elizabeth heard the salutation of Mary, the infant leaped in her womb: and Elizabeth was filled with the Holy Ghost, and she cried out with a loud voice and said : Blessed art thou among women ; and blessed is the fruit of thy womb. And whence is this to me, that the mother of my Lord should come to me (*Luke* i. 39–43)? And when Mary's days were accomplished that she should be delivered, she brought forth her firstborn son (*Luke* ii. 6, 7). And after eight days were accomplished that the child should be circumcised, his name was called Jesus, which was called by the angel, before he was conceived in the womb (21). And not long after, an angel of the Lord appeared in sleep to Joseph, saying: Arise, and take the child and his mother, and fly into Egypt; and be there until I shall tell thee. For it will come to pass that Herod will seek the child to destroy him (*Matt.* ii. 13). And at the marriage in Cana of Galilee, the wine failing, the mother of Jesus saith to him: They have no wine ; and she saith to the waiters: Whatsoever he shall say to you, do ye

(*John* ii. 1-5). And is it not written: There stood by the cross of Jesus, his mother and his mother's sister, Mary of Cleophas, and Mary Magdalene (*John* xix. 25)? Resting upon these reasons and these authorities, the Church cut off from her Communion those who, with heretical wickedness, should attempt to take away from the glory of Mary by denying that she was the mother of God (*Council of Ephesus, an.* 431).

II.

Mary, being the mother of God, is evidently exalted in dignity above all creatures. Although she is of most illustrious race, of the blood of the Patriarchs, and of the royal family of David, this is naught in comparison with the nobility, incomparably greater, which she acquires from her Son (*St. Pet. Damascen.*). The more noble the son is, the greater the honor of the mother; and the son of Mary being of infinite dignity and authority, the honor of his mother must be almost immeasurable. She alone can say with the eternal Father to the eternal Son: Thou art my son; this day have I begotten thee (*Is.* ii. 7). The Father says to Jesus, by the mouth of the Prophet: Thou art my son in virtue of eternal generation. Mary, by the Evangelist, says also to Jesus: Thou art my son in virtue of generation in time. And, as the tree is known by its fruits, the dignity of Mary, the mother of Jesus, is almost infinite (*Alb. Mag.*). Great is the elevation of Angels, Archangels, Thrones, Dominations, Powers, Cherubim, and Seraphim; but they are all far inferior to Mary. Great are the Patriarchs, the Prophets, the Apostles, the Martyrs, the Confessors but Mary is their Queen. Mary, says St. Gregory the Great, is the mountain of Isaias on the summit of the other mountains; for she transcends in loftiness of glory all angels and men. Mary is the silvery moon that illuminates by night the path of the traveler. Mary is the sun that by its effulgence eclipses the light of all the stars, and rules in splendor as if the stars had no existence. Fair as the moon, bright as the sun.

The intimate union also between Mary and God declares the sublimity of her dignity. Christ, the Son of God, received his human nature from Mary. By her divine maternity, therefore, Mary is most closely united with the infinite person of Christ; hence accrues to Mary a dignity almost infinite.

Mary, according to St. John Damascene,

by becoming the mother of the Creator, became at once the Queen of all creatures. Hence, says Gerson, there belongs to Mary a kind of natural dominion over the whole universe. All creatures, says St. Bernard, in whatever rank of being, whether merely spiritual, as angels; or rational, as men; or corporeal, as purely material beings; all in the heavens and on the earth, and in the places under the earth, that are subject to the omnipotent dominion of God, are subject also to the authority of the Holy Virgin Mary. The Church sanctions these assertions by saluting Mary as Queen of Heaven, Queen of Angels, Queen of the World.

ASPIRATION.

After this our exile, show us **Jesus, the** blessed fruit of thy womb.

PRACTICE.

Say your beads daily in honor of the Mother of God.

LITANY.

Read one of Cardinal Newman's Sermons on the Mother of God.

SIXTH DAY.

HOW WE SHOULD HONOR MARY OUR MOTHER.

"The valiant men ceased, and rested in Israel until Debbora arose, a mother arose in Israel."
Judges v. 7.

After the death of Aod, the children of Israel again did evil in the sight of the Lord; and the Lord delivered them up into the hands of Jabin, king of Chanaan, who reigned in Asor (*Judges* iv. 1, 2), and Asor subjected them for twenty years to all the hardships of servitude. Then the Lord bethought himself of his mercy to Israel, and raised up a woman to rule and deliver his people. She was Debbora, a prophetess, the wife of Lapidoth, and she sat under a palm tree which was called by her name, between Rama and Bethel, in Mount Ephraim; and the children of Israel came up to her for all judgment (*Judges* iv. 4, 5). So just were her judgments, and so mild and grateful her rule, that the people with acclamation saluted her as mother. The valiant men ceased and rested in Israel, until Debbora arose, a mother arose in Israel. This is an image of the vicissitudes which

should both sadden and rejoice the hearts
of men. Our first parents did evil in the
sight of God, and instead of preserving
for their children the sanctifying grace
which had been intrusted to them, they
transmitted to them a woful inheritance
of evils. We experience every day the
deadly effects of this inheritance. Our
understanding is darkened and our heart
is constantly exposed to the fury of a
thousand raging passions. But, thanks to
the goodness of God, if the tribes of Israel had, to comfort and rule them, their
mother, we have for our support and
guide a far greater mother than Debbora—Mary, the mother of God. Debbora
was only a passing figure of the glorious
Virgin who came to us in the fulness of
time. Debbora was a mother for a brief
period, and to the Israelites alone ; Mary
is a mother for all the children of men,
and for all the ages of eternity. She,
by addressing continual prayers to Jesus,
discharges the office of a mother in our regard, and she never fails to turn her countenance of love to him who with confidence invokes her aid.

I.

Whilst the prophecies were every moment receiving fulfilment, and the work

of man's redemption was approaching its consummation on Calvary, a most moving spectacle touched the loving heart of the Savior. Some holy women, who had ministered to him during the course of his preaching, and who would not abandon him in the extremity of his sufferings, stood near his cross. Amongst them Jesus beheld his mother, his tender mother whom a superhuman effort of love and courage had led to that mournful scene. The sight of her suffering Son fills her with desolation ; but faith in her Son, the Savior of the world, consoles her again ; and whilst the death of the Redeemer causes all nature to tremble, Mary looks on firm and immovable. Mary, at the foot of the cross, unites her heart with the heart of Jesus hanging on the cross, and well acquainted with the designs of Providence, she shares in spirit the sacrifice which is offered on Golgotha. Near his mother Jesus observes his beloved disciple, he who leaned on his breast at the last supper. At the sight of the two persons so dear to him, the Savior, though tortured with pain, exhausted, and humbled by the insults, the outrages and the blasphemies of his persecutors, gathers his energy, revives his tenderness, and gives them a final proof of his love, by making his last testament in their favor in the face of heaven and earth. But what can he bequeath them? He had not in life whereon to lay his head. His garments had been divided amongst his executioners, and his very blood had been poured out to the last drop. But his love discovered the means of leaving to each a precious legacy by bequeathing them mutually to each other. He saith to his mother, Woman, behold thy son. After that he saith to the disciple, Behold thy mother. And from that hour the disciple took her to his own (*John* xix. 26, 27). The Fathers recognize in the beloved disciple the representative of all the faithful whom the Savior loves with most tender and most perfect love. In the person of John we have been given to Mary as children, and Mary has been given to us as mother. It has been the will of God that Mary should adopt us as children, and he required of us that we should acknowledge her as mother.

Man may be considered under a twofold aspect, as regards the body, and as regards the soul. A twofold life is thus found in man: the one corporal, the other spiritual. Again the soul of man is to be considered, not only with reference to natural life, but much more with reference to supernatural life produced by sanctifying grace. On these grounds Richard of St. Lawrence thus reasons : If Eve is called the mother of the living, because from her descends to all men the life of nature, much more should Mary be called the mother of the living, because she is the mother of him from whom all receive the life of grace. St. Bernardine teaches, that when the Virgin gave her consent to the incarnation of the Lord, from that moment she bore us all spiritually in her bosom with all the affection of a most loving mother. One was the Son, says William of Paris, borne by the Virgin Mary, and he was the Savior of the world ; but in giving to the world him who is life, she brought forth many to the life of grace. Mary is then the mother of Christ by nature, and she is at the same time the mother of all Christians by grace.

II.

Mary is not only our mother in name, but she performs every day the part of a most loving mother. In the kingdom of glory she implores continually her Son in our behalf, for it is he who has consigned us to her as children. If Christ is our advocate with his Father, she is our advocate with her Son, Christ Jesus, our Savior. She is the mother of grace for the just man, that he may persevere and advance in the way of virtue; and she is the mother of mercy for the sinner who has the will to be converted to God. To all she says in the words of divine wisdom: I am the mother of fair love, and of fear, and of knowledge, and of holy hope. In me is all grace of the way and of the truth: in me is all hope of life and of virtue. Come over to me, all ye that desire me, and be filled with my fruits(*Eccl.* xxiv. 24, 26). Blessed is the man that heareth me, and that watcheth daily at my gates, and waiteth at the posts of my doors. He that shall find me shall find life, and shall have salvation from the Lord (*Prov.* viii. 34, 35). Mary, says one of her devout servants, loves us ardently because she adopted us as children, and wishes us to call her Mother of Love. No precept has been given to parents to love their children. This is a love of natural necessity. Wild beasts even are taught by nature to love their own offspring. Can a woman, says Isaias, forget her infant, so as not to have pity on the son of her womb ? And if she should forget, yet will not Mary forget us. She ardently desired to die with Jesus out of love for us, whom he so excessively loved. The Son was expiring on the cross, says St. Ambrose, and Mary was in spirit offering herself to die with him for our benefit.

The love of Mary for men arises from her love for God. The love of God and the love of our neighbor are embraced in the same precept. This commandment we have from God, that he who loveth God must love also his brother (1 *John* iv. 21). The more love for God increases, the more increases love for our neighbor. What did not an Alphonsus Liguori perform in the kingdom of Naples, a Charles Borromeo in the territory of Milan, or a Father Damian among the lepers? And why? Because they were inflamed with a strong and active love for God. But in love for God, Mary far excels all the Saints; therefore in love of her neighbor, Mary is more ardent and earnest than they were. Mary loves us because we are her children, given to her by the dying Savior. And she loves us fervently, because Jesus Christ has purchased us at the infinite price of his passion and death. She knows full well that her Son came into the world to seek and save that which was lost. She knows that Jesus Christ, although God, emptied himself, taking the form of a servant, being made in the likeness of men, and in habit found as a man ; that he humbled himself, becoming obedient unto death, even the death of the cross. Mary must then love those whom God loves ; and as God loves in order to save, and most ardently desires that we all be saved, Mary is for us a loving mother, whose whole solicitude is employed to conduct us to heaven.

ASPIRATION.

Show thyself a mother, O most sweet Virgin Mary.

PRACTICE.

On bended knees offer yourself to Mary as a child, and entreat her blessing.

LITANY.

Read a chapter of Father Müller's Devotion of the Holy Rosary.

SEVENTH DAY.

HOW WE SHOULD HONOR MARY OUR QUEEN.

"The king loved her more than all the women ; and he set the royal crown on her head, and made her queen instead of Vasthi." *Esther* ii. 17.

ASSUERUS having repudiated Vashti, sent persons all through the provinces, to look for beautiful maidens and virgins, and to conduct them to the city of Susan, that he might appoint the one who should please him most, in Queen Vashti's place. There was a man in the city of Susan, a Jew named Mardochai, who had under his protection a niece, named Esther, exceedingly fair and beautiful. She also, among the rest of the maidens, was delivered up, to be kept in the number of the women. And she pleased Assuerus and found favor in his sight. And the king loved her more than all the women ; and he set the royal crown on her head, and made her queen instead of Vasthi (*Esther* ii).

Many historical facts, recorded in Holy Writ, have an allegorical significance. In Assuerus God is shadowed forth, and in

Esther, the most blessed Virgin. As Assuerus preferred Esther to all others for her beauty, and elevated her to the condition of Queen of the Persians, so God loved Mary amongst all creatures for her sanctity, and exalted her to the rank of Queen of all Christians. To heighten our sentiments of respect and devotion for Mary, let us consider how greatly she is loved by God, and that God has crowned her in heaven as our Queen.

I.

The Scriptures and the Fathers of the Church teach us that God loved Mary above all created beings. In the book of Proverbs, Mary declares of herself, in the words applied to her by the Church—The Lord possessed me in the beginning of his ways, before he made anything from the beginning. I was set up from eternity, and of old before the world was made. The depths were not as yet, and I was already conceived ; neither had the fountains of waters as yet sprung up ; the mountains with their huge bulk had not as yet been established ; before the hills, I was brought forth. He had not as yet made the earth, nor the rivers, nor the poles of the world. From the beginning, and before the world, was I created. I was exalted like a cedar in Libanus, and as a cypress tree on Mount Sion. I was exalted like a palm tree in Cades, and as a rose plant in Jericho; and as a fair olive tree in the plains, and as a plane tree by the waters in the streets, was I exalted. I gave a sweet smell like cinnamon and aromatical balm; as the vine I have brought forth a pleasant odor, and my flowers are the fruit of honor and riches.

If from Proverbs and Ecclesiasticus we pass to the mystic book of Canticles, we find still more vividly expressed the love of God for the Holy Virgin; for it is the celestial Spouse himself who celebrates her praises. As the lily among thorns, so is my love among the daughters (*Cant.* ii. 2). Who is she that cometh forth as the morning rising, fair as the moon, bright as the sun, terrible as an army set in array (*Cant.* iv. 9)? The daughters saw her, and declared her most blessed; the queens praised her (vi. 8). Such are the various mystic expressions employed by Scripture to describe the especial love cherished by the Almighty for Mary, and the supreme complacency with which he has always regarded her. These expressions have indeed been turned into ridicule by the impious; but the sensual man perceiveth not the things that are of the spirit of God, for it is foolishness to him, and he cannot understand, but the spiritual man judgeth all things (1 Cor. ii. 14), for to him only is given the peace of God which surpasseth all understanding (Phil. iv. 7), whilst to the wicked it is utterly unknown.

To be convinced that Mary is dearer to Almighty God than all other creatures, it is sufficient to reflect that she has been called the first-born daughter of the Father, that she is the mother of the Son, and the spouse of the Holy Ghost. Mary says of herself, in the words of Ecclesiasticus: I came out of the mouth of the Most High, the first-born before all creatures (Eccl. xxiv. 5). God created her in the Holy Spirit, made her great in his sight, never suffered her to be sullied by sin, but preserved her from her conception pure and immaculate. The Blessed Virgin, says A Lapide, is the first amongst mere creatures: in her conception, nativity, sanctification, and glorification, God displayed his greatest power. God made in her as the first and most noble creature, an image of himself and of all his works, that in her he might always and by all beings be praised and glorified. God loved Mary with especial love because he designed her to be the Mother of his only-begotten Son. This is an honor which exalts Mary above all the excellence of creatures, visible and invisible, whether they be considered separately or all combined. In view of this dignity, God conceived her distinctly in his mind, and chose her from all eternity, and adorned her with holiness, and beautified her with every virtue, that she might be rendered worthy to be his mother. This dignity being reserved for her alone, is it surprising that God should love her above all creatures? Mary is the spouse of the Holy Ghost. How great, then, must be the love of God for Mary! It has been announced that God sanctified his tabernacle, that holiness belonged to his abode, and that he who would create it would repose in it. This was accomplished when the Angel said to Mary : The Holy Ghost shall come upon thee, and the power of the Most High shall overshadow thee. And therefore, also, the Holy which shall be born of thee shall be called the Son of God (*Luke* i. 35). And Mary replied : Behold the handmaid of the Lord ; be it done to me according to thy word (38).

Then, says St. Athanasius, the Holy Ghost descended upon her in the plenitude of his virtues, and bestowed upon her the fulness of grace. The Blessed Virgin, writes Albertus Magnus, was full of grace, because she possessed in the highest degree the general and special graces communicated to all creatures; because she possessed those graces of which every other creature is destitute; because her grace was so great that greater could not be imparted to any mere creature; because grace uncreated, which is God, she embraced wholly within herself.

It is true therefore, that if Esther was beloved by Assuerus above the other maidens for her beauty, Mary was beloved by Almighty God above all other creatures for her sanctity, so that the Father cherished her as his most beloved daughter, the Son as his most worthy mother, and the Holy Ghost as his immaculate spouse.

II.

Mary enjoyed to the utmost extent the predilection of that God who is the bestower of every good gift, and he elevated her to the sublime dignity of Queen of heaven and earth. David saw her with prophetic vision, and exclaimed: The

Queen stood on thy right hand in gilded clothing, surrounded with variety (*Ps.* xliv. 9). God placed upon her head a crown of glory upon the mitre, wherein was engraved holiness, an ornament of honor; a work of power, and delightful to the eyes for its beauty (*Eccl.* xlv. 14). The Lord girded her about with a glorious girdle, and clothed her with a robe of glory: and crowned her with majestic attire (xlv. 9). All the glory of the King's daughter is within. The daughters of Tyre with their gifts, all the rich among the people, shall entreat her countenance (*Ps.* xliv. 13, 14). In the Canticle of Canticles it is written of Mary: Come from Libanus, my spouse, come from Libanus, come ; thou shalt be crowned (*Can.* iv. 8). The daughters saw her, and declared her most blessed ; the queens praised her (vi. 8).

And what say the Fathers of the Church ? If the Son is king, says St. Athanasius, the mother is really and truly queen. Mary, says St. Bernardine, merited the dominion of the world and the sceptre of the universe, from the moment that she gave her consent to the Incarnation of the Word. One, writes Arnoldus Abbot, is the flesh of Mary and Christ, one the spirit, one the charity.

From the time it was said to Mary,—the
Lord is with thee, the promise and the
gift remained inseparably united. Unity
admits of no division. I esteem the glory
of the Son, not only common to the
mother, but, in a certain manner, the same
with the glory of the mother. Hence, the
mother cannot be excluded from the
dominion and power of the son. We cannot more effectually invoke Mary, says
Gerson, than by calling upon her as
mother of God; for by this title she
claims a kind of authority and dominion
over the Lord of the whole world; with
greater wisdom, then, over all that is subjected to him. Therefore, concludes St.
John Damascene, the mother is truly and
undoubtedly the sovereign and mistress
of all created beings.

But when was Mary crowned Queen of
heaven and earth ? On the day of her assumption. On that day the glorious Virgin
ascended the heavens, and, ineffably exalted, commenced her eternal reign. On
that day she was placed at the right hand
of the Father. Thus constituted Queen,
she possesses by right the empire of the
universe in union with her Son. The creatures which serve the most Holy Trinity
serve also the glorious Virgin. Angels
and men, all creatures in the heavens and

on earth, because all are subjected to the dominion of God, are subject also to Mary (*St. Bernard. Senen.*). Mary is styled Queen of heaven because she excels saints and angels in glory, dignity, and authority. She is styled Queen of the earth because she concurs with her Son, the Lord of the earth, in the government of men and of earthly events. Continue then, O Mary, writes one of her devout servants, continue to govern and to dispose of what belongs to thy Son. Act with confidence, for thou art Queen, the mother of the King and his spouse.

ASPIRATION.

Glorious Queen of the World, intercede for us with the Lord.

PRACTICE.

Repeat frequently : Hail Mary, full of grace.

LITANY.

Read "The Hail Mary" by J. P. Val d' Eremao, D. D.

EIGHTH DAY.

HOW WE SHOULD HONOR MARY QUEEN OF MERCY.

"What wilt thou, Queen Esther? What is thy request? If thou shouldst even ask one half of the kingdom it shall be given to thee."*Esther* v. 3.

AFTER Esther found favor in the sight of Assuerus, and had the royal crown set upon her head, better days seemed to rise for the Hebrews, and the severity of the servitude under which they had groaned in the Persian empire seemed to be mitigated. But suddenly a furious tempest arose, which threatened with total ruin that unfortunate people. The impious Aman, not satisfied with being seated above all the satraps and princes of Persia, and with receiving honor from the people second only to that exhibited to the king, urged on by hatred, swore enmity against all the Jews; and he succeeded in having an edict hung up in Susan, and promulgated throughout the empire, commanding that all the Jews, both young and old, little children and women, should be killed and destroyed in one day. When Mardochai had heard these things, he rent his garments, and put on sackcloth, strewing ashes on his head ; and he cried with a loud voice in the street in the midst of the city, showing the anguish of his mind ; and in all provinces, towns, and places to which the king's cruel edict was come, there was great mourning among the Jews. Esther, at the urgent solicitation of Mardochai, presented herself before the king, to crave mercy for her people. And when the king saw Esther standing, he said to her: What wilt thou, Queen Esther ? What is thy request?   If thou shouldst even ask one half of the kingdom, it shall be given to thee.   Then Queen Esther answered: If I have found favor in thy sight, O King, and if it please thee, give me my life, for which I ask, and my people for which I request : for we are given up, I and my people, to be destroyed, to be slain, and to perish.   The petition of Esther was granted and the edict of destruction was recalled.   The joyful event was brought about by the intercession of the compassionate Esther. In reading Esther, who does not immediately turn his thoughts to Mary? Esther is one of the types of the most blessed Virgin. As Esther soothed the anger of Assuerus, and liberated her nation from destruction, so Mary, by the loveliness of her virtues, rendered the Almighty so favorable, that besides choosing her as his mother, he wished her to be a peacemaker for the human race, and the dispenser of his mercies. In this sentiment the Church salutes her: Hail, holy queen, mother of mercy ! Having already considered that she is our queen, let us consider to-day that she is the Queen of Mercy, and let us reflect that she employs her mercy in favor of the just man and the sinner.

I.

If the Virgin of Nazareth, as the Fathers agree, by consenting to the Incarnation of the Word, merited the supremacy of the world; if he who was born of her is king, and his mother should be reputed as queen ; if the mother cannot be excluded from the domination of her son; if the regal glory is not only common between mother and son, but is almost identical in both; then Mary must be esteemed as justly and truly our queen. And Mary is not only our queen, but she is a queen amiable, clement, faithful beyond measure, who has always in view the happiness of the afflicted children of Adam. Hail, Holy Queen, Mother of mercy.

In the opinion of Albertus Magnus, the

very name of queen includes in its signification care and compassion for the poor.
The greatness and magnificence of a ruler,
as Seneca says, exhibit themselves in the
timely succor ministered to the miserable.
A usurper has always his own interests
in view ; but a lawful ruler seeks to
promote the welfare and happiness of
his subjects.   When Saul was chosen
king of the people of Israel, the Almighty
commanded his prophet to anoint him
and sanctify him with oil, which is a
symbol of mercy and compassion, that
he might understand that he should be
the father of his people, and that, like a
father, he should cultivate in his heart
sentiments of kindness and beneficence
towards all his subjects. According to
the Psalmist (*Ps.* lxxi.), the sovereign
authority of Almighty God is exercised
in justice and mercy. With justice he
judges all men, and inflicts upon the
wicked the punishment deserved by their
crimes.   With mercy he grants salvation
to the righteous.   And thus he recom-
penses every one according to his works.
The Blessed Virgin, says St. Thomas,
by conceiving in her womb the Son of
God and afterwards giving him birth, obtained one half of the kingdom of God,
so that she is the queen of mercy, whilst

Christ is the king of justice. Isaias had before prophesied that God would prepare his throne in mercy. But what throne has God established in mercy? St. Bonaventure replies, that throne of the divine mercy is Mary, the mother of mercy, in whom all men found the relief of mercy. As we have a most merciful Father, so we have a most merciful Mother. If the Lord our God is sweet and mild, and plenteous in mercy to all that call upon him, our Queen also is good, beneficent, patient, and of great mercy, propitiously accepting our prayers, and turning an attentive ear to the voice of our supplications.

If we read the scriptures with care, and inquire into the object for which Almighty God, by ways so opposite and extraordinary, elevated Joseph to the highest dignities of Egypt, we discover that it was none other than the salvation of his people.

In like manner we poor sinners address Mary our Queen in our own behalf. Think not, O Mary, that God has crowned thee Queen of the world solely that thou mightest consult thy own interest. He has exalted thee, that thou, being made so great, mightest feel a more lively compassion for unhappy mortals, and exert thyself more effectually to alleviate their sorrows.

But who can call in doubt the mercy of Mary? Who is ignorant that she is the mother of fair love and holy hope? Has not the Lord by countless figures indicated the mercy of his most holy mother? St. Fulgentius calls Mary the opening into heaven, because through her the Almighty poured forth the light of truth over all ages. He calls her the ladder of heaven, because through her God descended to the earth, and men may merit to ascend to heaven. He only will be allowed to ascend, who will believe that the Son of God descended to the earth and appeared in human form through the ever-glorious Virgin Mary. St. Bernardine teaches that Mary is the rainbow set in the clouds, a sign of the everlasting covenant that all flesh shall no more be overwhelmed with destruction.

And how great was the love of the Heavenly Father, when Mary exclaimed: My soul doth magnify the Lord ; and my spirit hath rejoiced in God my Savior. As Abigail was a figure of Mary, so David was a figure of our Lord. David was offended by the foolish Nabal, and God is insulted by the sinner. David was appeased by Abigail, and God is appeased by Mary. Abigail restrained the temporal vengeance of David, and soothed him by gifts and entreaties; Mary extinguishes the eternal vengeance of God by her prayers and her merits (*St. Bonav.*). No one, says St. Bernard, is so fit to extend the hand in order to arrest the sword of divine vengeance unsheathed against the sinner, as thou, O Virgin, replete with divine love, by whose means the merits of the passion of the Son are applied to us, and we receive mercy from the treasures of God our Lord. Mary is not, therefore, only our queen, but she is also queen of mercy.

II.

If we consider in favor of whom Mary exercises her mercy, we find that she exercises it for the just that they may persevere, and for sinners that they may be converted to God. She employs it also for our temporal as well as our spiritual good. Moses relates (*Gen.* iv.) that God, seeing that the wickedness of men was great on the earth, repented himself that he had made man on the earth. And being touched inwardly with sorrow of heart, he said, I will destroy man, whom

I have created, from the face of the earth. And he commanded Noe to construct an ark of timber planks and to prepare it for the reception of the men and of the living things that were to be preserved from the fury of the destroying waters Eight persons of the family of Noe, and the animals necessary for the propagation of the different species, were saved by the ark from the waters of the deluge. St. Bernard, St. John of Damascus, and St. Bonaventure, teach us that the ark was a figure of Mary, that, as by means of the ark, the eight persons and the animals in the ark escaped destruction, so the just, represented by the inmates of the ark, attain salvation by means of Mary. It is an article of our faith that no one is saved without the concurrence of divine grace ; and that a special assistance of God is necessary for perseverance in justice. This grace we obtain by means of Jesus Christ, who died, and who rose also again, who is at the right hand of God, who also maketh intercession for us. Mary can wish only what Christ Jesus wishes; but Christ wishes nothing but mercy. Mary therefore uses mercy with the just, and entreats God to grant them the graces necessary for perseverance.

Mary has equal care for sinners. As a

fond mother, if she sees her little child weeping or suffering from a wound, hastens to wipe away its tears and to bind up its wound, so the tender mother Mary never desists from her supplications to her Son in favor of the sinner, until the wounds made in the soul by sin are bound up and healed. Who ever invoked Mary without being heard? Who ever craved her patronage and received a refusal? It appears to be an established law of providence that mercy shall be shown to all those for whom Mary intercedes. The law of clemency is on her tongue (*Prov.* xxxi. 26). St. Bernard, inquiring of himself why the Church invokes Mary by the sublime title of Queen of Mercy, replies, that this is done that we may firmly believe that Mary throws open the treasury of the divine mercy to whom she pleases, and as she pleases. So that the sinner can never be lost if Mary protects him. The repentant sinner is never rejected by Mary. However numerous may be his crimes, however frightful their deformity, if he breathes with confidence at the feet of Mary one heartfelt sigh of sorrow, she instantly extends her merciful hand and withdraws him from the precipice of despair, and never abandons him until she beholds him reconciled with

God. Mary seeks our temporal and spiritual welfare.   She is the mother and the protectress of the human family. She is a physician for the infirm, a guide for the wealthy, consolation for the desolate. Her holy and devout servants have entitled her the gate of heaven, the glory of the human race, the refuge of sinners, the support of the elect, the fountain of graces, the harbor of the shipwrecked, the shield of the combatants, the mother of orphans, the protection of widows, the advocate of penitents, the prototype of the just, the hope and glory of Christians, the title of honor of Catholics.   I shall conclude with St. Anastasius Sinaite, by exhorting the Jew, the Greek, and the Gentile, all men indeed, to seek and find that mother of mercy whom the Lord created for the assistance of the whole human race. Them that seek her she introduces into the kingdom of God ; and, by rendering them children of light, gives birth to heirs of the kingdom of heaven.

ASPIRATION.

From all sin deliver us, Mother of Mercy.

PRACTICE.

Call frequently upon the name of Jesus and Mary. By honoring Jesus we honor Mary. By honoring Mary we honor Jesus.

LITANY.

Read Chapter II. of St. Luke.

NINTH DAY.

HOW WE SHOULD HONOR MARY QUEEN OF ANGELS.

"And there appeared a great wonder in heaven ; a woman clothed with the sun, and the moon under her feet, and on her head a crown of twelve stars." *Apoc.* xii. 1.

WHEN we meditate attentively upon the books of the Prophets of God, our minds become so excited, that we seem to be living in their midst in the remote days of the ancient law, and to see them waking their harmonious harps, throwing themselves in song into the hearts of future ages, celebrating with hymns of exultation the mercies of God. In them everything inspires a sacred awe, because everything in them is grandeur, sublimity, mystery. But our feeling of awe is greatly increased when we turn our thoughts to the Apocalypse of St. John, the Apostle. As the noble eagle disdains the lowly valleys, and builds his nest on the summit of precipitous cliffs, unknown to footstep of man and unvisited by birds of humbler flight, and, spreading his vigorous wings, emulates the swiftness of the wind, buries himself in the remoteness of space, and gazes with undazzled eye in the face of the sun, so St. John, more sublime than the other Prophets, and more profound than the other Evangelists, soared so high that he reached the fountain source from which all things descend. Being exiled by Domitian to the barren and solitary island of Patmos, and there continually absorbed in divine meditations, God presented to his mind various spectacles, sometimes joyful, sometimes afflicting. Amongst these was a most extraordinary prodigy that became visible in heaven. And what was this? There appeared a great wonder in heaven; a woman clothed with the sun, and the moon under her feet, and on her head a crown of twelve stars. But what is the mystery of this vision? Albertus Magnus recognizes in that woman the great Virgin Mary, triumphant in Paradise, and honored by all the angels and saints. The spouse of the Canticles, alluding· to the glory of Mary, says that she is as fair as the moon, bright as the sun. The Church asserts of her, that on the day of her assumption she was exalted above the choirs of the angels in the heavens, and salutes her as Queen of the Heavens, Sovereign of the Angels. Let us now consider in what manner Mary is queen of the angels, and how she has been honored by them as such.

I.

Jesus Christ, the **Holy of Holies**, and King of kings, is the head, not only of men, but also of the angels. The fulness of grace in Christ is the cause of all the graces which are found in intelligent creatures. The angels receive grace and glory from Christ, and acknowledge him as their king and head ; they consequently acknowledge as their queen the Blessed Virgin Mary,·his most glorious mother. The Blessed Virgin is not only queen of the angels, but she may, in a certain sense, be justly called their mother. The angels receive illumination and the perfection of beatitude from Christ, by whom all things are restored in heaven and on earth ; therefore the most Blessed Virgin, the mother of Christ, is the cause in a measure of the glory of the angels, and may be appropriately called their mother.

Mary is the true mother of God ; the angels are but his servants; therefore she is so much better than the angels, as she has inherited a more excellent name above them. To none of the angels, but to Jesus Christ alone, has God the Father said, Thou art my Son; this day have I begotten thee (*Heb.* i. 5). Which of the angels can say to the Redeemer and Savior of man : Thou art my Son ? It is enough for them, and they deem it a high honor that, being spirits by nature, they are made angels by grace (*Ps.* ciii. 4). Mary, on the contrary, knowing that she is the mother of Him before whose infinite majesty the angels prostrate themselves in adoration, says to him confidently and fearlessly: Thou art my Son. There is an immense difference, concludes St. John Damascene, between the mother of God and the servants of God. Rightfully, therefore, is Mary called Queen of Angels.

Mary is not only queen of the angels but she immeasurably exceeds them in **grace**. St. Gregory the Great and many

others teach us that angels are divided
into nine orders or choirs. They form
three hierarchies, each of which com-
prises three choirs. The first hierarchy
embraces the Seraphim, the Cherubim,
the Thrones;the second,the Dominations,
the Virtues, and the Powers; the third,
the Principalities, the Archangels, and
the Angels. Their different names arise
from the different offices for which they
are destined.

The Seraphim are so denominated
from the divine love with which they are
inflamed, and which they transfuse into
others. But can any creature love God
more ardently than Mary did? The fervor of Mary's love was symbolized in the
bush that burned without being consumed; so says St. Bonaventure. The
love which she bore her son was an infinite love,in the opinion of St. Bernardine.
The greater the purity of heart, the
greater the love,argues Albertus Magnus;
but Mary possessed purity of heart in the
highest degree ; therefore her love for
God was of the utmost intensity, and
greater cannot be found in created
beings. Mary alone was saluted as full
of grace; but grace is the daughter of
divine love. Mary, says Richard of St.
Victor, desired the salvation of all ; she

sought for it, and obtained it; indeed, she herself, by giving birth to the Savior, became salvation for all. Mary then loved God more than the Seraphim, and transfused her love into others. She is Queen of the Seraphim !

The Cherubim are so called from the knowledge with which they are adorned, and which they communicate to others. But the Blessed Virgin was adorned with the most eminent knowledge, by which she penetrated the abyss of divine wisdom, bearing in her bosom him in whom are hidden all the treasures of wisdom and knowledge. She is Queen of the Cherubim !

The Thrones are so named, because in them is seated the divine majesty as judge, and through them the divine judgments are announced to other angels. But Mary is more exalted than the Thrones, because she is the real abode in which wisdom incarnate dwelt, the temple of the Holy Ghost, and the august throne of the three divine persons, and in her the great work of the redemption of man commenced. Queen of Thrones is Mary then !

In the Dominations appears in the highest degree the supreme dominion of God over created things, and they hold

dominion over the inferior angels. But
Mary presides over all the angelic choirs;
she commands them, as a lady her servants, as a queen her subjects. The Dominations are obedient to her commands
regarding the salvation of men, and find
greater pleasure in serving her than in
exercising dominion. Hail ! Queen of the
Dominations !

The Virtues, being invested with divine
efficiency, watch over the general laws of
the universe, and operate wonders both
in the order of nature and of grace. But
do not the Fathers esteem Mary herself
a celestial prodigy, a most extraordinary
wonder of the universe? It is something
altogether new, says St. Epiphanius, to
see in heaven a woman clothed with the
sun. It is astonishing beyond measure
that the creature should have become
mother of the Creator, and have borne in
her bosom him whom the heavens cannot
contain. It is an incomprehensible miracle, that the Lord of the angels should
have become the son of a virgin, and
that, at her breast, he should have been
nourished, who feeds the fowls of the air
and the fishes of the sea and the animals
of the forest, and arrays in beauty the
flowers of the mead. And what part of
the world, moreover, has not witnessed

the miraculous power of the Virgin ? Mary, therefore, is Queen of the Virtues!

The Powers participate in the mightiness of God, and curbing the audacity of the malignant spirits, render them harmless to mortals. But Mary crushed the head of the infernal serpent. Woe to us if Mary's maternal kindness did not discover to us the arts and wiles and snares of the envious spirits of the abyss! Woe to us if we were not animated and strengthened by her in the combats of the spirit! Mary is Queen of the Powers!

To the Principalities Almighty God consigns the guardianship of all rulers and governments. But the Blessed Virgin had the guardianship of the King of kings; and he was respectfully subject to her (*Luke* ii. 51). To Mary are applied the words of divine wisdom : In every nation I have the chief rule (*Eccl.* xxiv. 10). By me kings reign, and lawgivers decree just things; by me princes rule, and the mighty decree justice (*Prov.* viii. 15, 16). Mary has also under her patronage the universal Church—defends it, protects it, and crushes with her foot the hydra of heresy. Mary is Queen of the Principalities!

The Archangels announce to men affairs of moment, and are guardians of pontiffs, kings, princes, and others in authority. Upon thy walls, O Jerusalem, says Isaias, I have appointed watchmen all the day and all the night (*Is.* lxxii. 6). But the Holy Virgin is the guardian of all cities and of churches. Earthly potentates have committed their kingdoms and their newly-founded cities to the protection of Mary. There is no Catholic kingdom or government or city, where temples, altars, statues, and images, do not attest that the patronage of Mary is, and has been, earnestly invoked. Justly then is Mary called Queen of Archangels!

To the Angels is intrusted the office of guarding and protecting men individually considered. But Mary was the guardian and protectress of God made man! When Herod, enraged at the coming of the Messias, wished to imbrue his hands in his blood, she fled with her child and took shelter in Egypt, thus preserving him from the vengeance of that sanguinary king. Each of the angels is appointed to watch over one man alone ; but Mary has charge of all men together and of every one in particular ; for she is the mother and sovereign of all men, and looks upon them all as her servants and children. The angels announce to men the things of heaven ; Mary discharges this office in a manner far more sublime than they. Hail, Mary, Queen of Angels! exalted above them all in grace and glory! All the angelic choirs bow before thee in awe and veneration, and sing ever the praises of their sovereign Queen.

II.

But what devout homage have angels exhibited to Mary? They so venerated her that we may address to her, as proceeding from them, the words recorded in holy writ: We are thy servants; whatsoever thou shalt command us we will do (4 *Kings* x. 5). In developing this second part we shall adhere closely to the Scriptures and the Fathers.

St. Vincent Ferreri, speaking of the conception of the Blessed Virgin, and calling it light, because it was free from every shade of sin, thus expresses himself: As soon as the soul of Mary was created it was sanctified, and immediately the angels in heaven celebrated the feast of her conception. Therefore does David sing, Light is risen to the just, and joy to the right of heart (*Ps.* xcvi. 11). Light to Christ whose mother Mary is to be; **joy to the angels who were never stained** with sin. This was the first honor shown to Mary by the angels in heaven. At her birth the princes of heaven, dazzled by her effulgence, exclaimed, Who is she that cometh forth as the morning rising, fair as the moon, bright as the sun (*Cant.* iv. 9) ? And learning by divine illustration who she was, they bowed low in reverence in presence of her glory, and immediately intoning a canticle of praise to the Son of God and his future mother, drew forth from the divine treasury the name of Mary, and conveyed it from heaven to earth. When the time for the fulfilment of the prophecies arrived, the celestial messenger, who announced to her that she was to become the mother of God, could not have pronounced upon her a higher encomium than he did by saying, Hail, full of grace, the Lord is with thee; blessed art thou among women. Fear not, Mary, for thou hast found grace with God. The Holy Ghost shall come upon thee ; and the power of the Most High shall overshadow thee. And therefore also the Holy which shall be born of thee, shall be called the Son of God.   In the anxiety of mind caused by the persecution of Herod, it is the opinion of the Fathers that Mary and Joseph had angels to console them and accompany them in their flight into Egypt and defend them from every danger. When Mary, after her death, was taken up into heaven in body and soul, the angels received her with acclamations and conducted her in triumph to the throne of God to be crowned queen of saints and angels, of heaven and earth. Let us then sing with the Church: The Holy mother of God is exalted above all the choirs of angels to the heavenly kingdom; and devoutly exclaim with St. Athanasius: Thee all the celestial and terrestrial hierarchies proclaim blessed; and raising their hands on high, bless thee who art blessed in heaven, and on earth hailed as blessed.

ASPIRATION.

From the snares of the enemy free us, Holy Virgin Mary.

PRACTICE.

In every temptation, call without delay upon the name of Mary.

LITANY.

Read Month of Mary by Father Beckx, S.J.

TENTH DAY.

HOW WE SHOULD HONOR MARY QUEEN OF ALL THE SAINTS.

"And in the last day the mountain of the house of the Lord shall be prepared, on the top of the mountains, and it shall be exalted above the hills ; and all nations shall flow unto it." *Is.* ii. 2.

GREAT and wonderful is God ! And although the Hebrew nation was slow of understanding, stiff-necked, rebellious and disloyal, still, through his prophets, the Lord aroused their sluggish imaginations, and softened their stubborn hearts, by describing in symbols and figures the future magnificence of his religion. Filled with the spirit of God, the son of Amos lifted up his prophetic voice and sang, In the last day the mountain of the house of the Lord shall be prepared on the top of mountains, and it shall be exalted above the hills; and all nations shall flow unto it. And many people shall go and say, Come and let us go up to the mountain of the Lord, and to the house of the God of Jacob, and he will teach us his ways, and we will walk in his paths ; for the law shall come forth from

Sion, and the word of the Lord from Jerusalem. Thus prophesied Isaias of the future Savior of man—the Messias; foretelling his mercies, and the salutary changes which would be wrought amongst men by his appearance on earth. St. Gregory the Great, commenting on this passage of Isaias, writes as follows: By this mountain may be also designated the most Blessed Virgin Mary; for she, by the dignity of her election, transcended the loftiness of every other most favored creature. Was not Mary an elevated mountain, who, to be prepared to conceive the eternal word, exalted the summit of her merits above all the choirs of angels to the very throne of Eternity itself? The Virgin is that mountain, says St. John Damascene, which rises sublime above every mountain and hill, above angels and men, the mountain in which God was pleased to dwell. Mary is queen of all the saints, and as such the Church solemnly invokes her. In what manner is Mary queen of all the saints on earth and in heaven?

I.

The supreme ruler of all kingdoms condescending to the desire of the Hebrews demanding a king, selected for this office Saul. And there was not among the children of Israel a goodlier person than he; from his shoulders and upward, he appeared above all the people. The Almighty, wishing to give a queen to angels and men, sought for a woman who should rise above all others in abundance of grace and multiplicity of merits. The favored one was Mary, who was so copiously replenished with merits and graces, and afterward exalted to glory so sublime that she far surpasses all the other saints in merit, grace and glory. The Blessed Virgin, then, not only exceeds in dignity the angelic spirits, but, like the moon in the midst of the stars, shines a queen amongst all the saints.

Next to the angels the Church ranks the Patriarchs. Mary is their queen; for she possessed all their gifts in a higher degree, all their virtues, all their merits, and eclipsed all their most brilliant achievements. The most striking virtue of those holy men was faith. This is the lamp which, placed on the top of a mountain, throws light over the distant slopes and plains. Faith is the basis of every virtue, the foundation of the life of the true believer. Without it, it is impossible to please God. Faith is the wisdom

that subjugates the world. To it should
we firmly cling ; according to it should
we act.   It is certain that the providence
of God disposes, guides, and governs all
things ; so that not a leaf falls from the
tree, not a sparrow from the sky, without his pleasure. To him, therefore,
should we wholly commit ourselves, fully
confident that we shall receive from his
hands timely aid. In this manner acted
Abraham, who, when commanded to
sacrifice his son Isaac, although he saw
the course of the promise of God inter-
rupted by this command and his own
hopes deluded, still did not hesitate in
faith. And he learned by experience
that God alone saves those who hope in
him, and that without him there is no
powerful help nor useful counsel nor
enduring providence. The faith of Abraham was a subject of admiration to after
generations. So were the trials of Jacob,
the innocence of Joseph, the strength of
Samson, the patience of Job, the zeal of
Elias, the justice of David, and the wisdom of Solomon. But whatever existed
in them of grace and virtue, whatever
praises were pronounced of them, whatever they heroically performed, we find
combined in Mary. Hence, by St. Lawrence Giustiniani she is called the vivid

exemplar of every virtue. The Blessed Virgin is therefore Queen of the Patriarchs, whether we regard her birth, she being of their race, or all the gifts of grace which she received from Almighty God. She is crowned with a double diadem; one she inherits as daughter from her ancestors, the other, as mother she receives from her Son.

The Church, after the Patriarchs, contemplates the Prophets. They are so named, because, by divine revelation or inspiration, they foresaw future events and foretold specifically their accomplishment. To foresee and foretell future events is an eminent favor of the Holy Ghost. But Mary alone received the fulness of the Holy Ghost. Therefore she is greater than all the prophets. Mary was saluted by the angel as full of grace. She was assured that the Holy Ghost should come upon her, and that the virtue of the Most High should overshadow her (*Luke* i. 35). The Virgin is, moreover, called by the Church the seat of wisdom. The mind, therefore, of the Blessed Virgin was replenished by the infinite wisdom of God with light so abundant that she read in its brightness the past, the present, and the future.

But when did Mary receive the spirit

of Prophecy, and where are her predictions? She acquired the prophetic spirit when she was full of grace and overshadowed by the virtue of the Most High. She manifested the gift of prophecy when she foretold that all generations should call her blessed (*Luke* i. 48). She is then Queen of the Prophets!

Mary is styled by the Church Queen of Apostles. The Apostles were called by the Redeemer the light of the world. You are the light of the world (*Matt.* v. 14). To Mary belongs a more magnificent title. She may be called the Sun of the world; because she enlightens those who are sitting in darkness and the shadow of death, and leads them to the attainment of divine grace. According to St. Jerome, the name apostle is also interpreted master, instructor. But Mary is regarded by the fathers as instructor of the apostles, as enlightener of the nations (*St. Aug.*). We are taught by St. Thomas of Villanova that, after the death of Jesus, the apostles assembled in the room of the last supper, in company with Mary, and sought from her consolation and instruction. To Mary then justly belongs the title of Queen of Apostles.

The Martyrs endured persecution and

death ; but more cruel and more multiplied were the sufferings of Mary. To
her the temple of Jerusalem was what
Gethsemani was to her Son. Faithfully
obedient to the law, she presented her
infant to the Lord. Simeon seeing the
Christ of the Lord and his mother exclaimed : Behold this child is set for the
ruin and for the resurrection of many in
Israel, and for a sign which shall be con-
tradicted ; and thy own soul a sword shall
pierce (*Luke* ii. 34, 35). How great was the
affliction of Mary's heart when Herod
was seeking the Child to destroy him.
How great was her anxiety when the
child Jesus remained in Jerusalem, and
for three days she sought him sorrowing
(*Luke* ii. 48). But her anguish who
can express when Christ was betrayed
by Judas, was captured by the Jews, insulted by the princes of the synagogue,
scourged at the pillar, crowned with
thorns, overwhelmed by the weight of
the cross ; when, for three hours, he
hung in agony between heaven and earth,
and finally expired ? Nothing but a miracle of Omnipotence could have sustained our mother in her sorrows. St.
Bernardine assures us that the afflictions
of Mary's tender, loving soul, distributed
amongst all creatures, would have caused

the immediate death of every living being.

St. Jerome names Confessors those who
confess with the tongue the truths of the
faith of Christianity, lead a holy life according to them, and at last depart in the
Lord. But who ignores that Mary excelled
all the saints in the practice of every
Christian virtue, and served them all as
a guide? They, by imitating her example, were great in humility, rich in
poverty, sovereigns in obedience, angels in the flesh, heroes in persecution,
sublime in prayer, and resplendent with
every virtue. Mary, therefore, having excelled on earth in grace and virtue the
Patriarchs, the Prophets, the Apostles,
the Martyrs, and the Confessors, is to be
saluted as Queen of all Saints!

II.

But there are other powerful reasons
which authorize the devout children of
Mary to proclaim her Queen of all the
Saints, namely the glory which Mary enjoys in heaven, and the patronage which,
above all the saints, she extends to all the
afflicted children of Adam. St. Peter, in
the name of the Apostles, said to the Redeemer: Behold, we have left all things and
have followed thee : what, therefore, shall

we have? And Jesus said to them : Amen,
I say to you, that you who have followed
me in the regeneration, when the Son of
man shall sit in the seat of his majesty,
you also shall sit on twelve seats
judging the twelve tribes of Israel (*Matt.*
xix. 27, 28). The apostles, for having renounced all things and followed Jesus, are
seated in heaven. Will not Mary possess
a seat brighter, more elevated than all
the apostles? If a throne was set for the
mother of Solomon, and she sat on his
right hand (3 *Kings* ii. 19), is Mary held in
less esteem by Almighty God? Is she not
the mother of the King of kings ? She is
then Queen of all the Saints! If, besides,
the glory of the Saints is in proportion to
the merits gained and the graces received,
Mary, surpassing beyond measure all
the Saints in merit and grace, enjoys
greater glory and merit than they ; she
is therefore their Queen. In the opinion of St. Bernardine, the glory of
Mary differs as much from the glory of
all the other Blessed as the sun differs
from the other celestial bodies ; as they
are illumined by the sun, so the whole
celestial court is made bright by the
brilliancy of Mary's glory.

Mary, as mother of Jesus, possessing
immense treasures of merit and grace, is

much more powerful for our benefit than every other saint. The other saints, says Idiota, by right of protection, can render greater assistance in heaven to those who are particularly assigned to their care; but the Blessed Virgin, as their queen, is patroness and advocate of all Christians, and is equally solicitous for the welfare of all her subjects (*Idiota de Contempl. Virg.*). Do you fear, O sinner, on account of your wickedness and your crimes, to approach the throne of the eternal Father?   This should not be: for the Father has his son Jesus as a mediator between himself and man.   Do you wish to have an advocate with Jesus Christ? Implore the patronage of Mary. No tongue could enumerate the beneficent acts of Mary; for they are almost infinite in number.   Favors and graces the greatest, the most remarkable, the most rare, when asked of her with humility of heart, have been readily obtained. Through recourse to her, sight has been restored to the blind, speech to the dumb; the lame have been made to walk; lepers have been cleansed; and the possessed have been liberated from the power of the devil. The favors imparted by Mary to men are more numerous than the drops of water in the ocean, the leaves in the forest, and the grains of sand on the sea shore. Hence, with unanimous assent, Europe, Asia, Africa and America, proclaim Mary Queen of all the Saints, because she more freely and abundantly than all the others distributes her benefits to the children of men.

ASPIRATION.

In thee above all others did Christ our Savior find delight.

PRACTICE.

Thank God for the singular favors bestowed upon the Blessed Virgin.

LITANY.

Read Litany of Loretto by Archbishop Kenrick.

ELEVENTH DAY.

HOW TO HONOR MARY COÖPERATING IN OUR REDEMPTION.

"I will put enmities between thee and the woman, and thy seed and her seed: she shall crush thy head." *Gen.* iii. 13.

AFTER God had created the heavens and the earth and set in order the whole universe, one being, the most admirable in nature, still remained unmade. This being was man; and God made him to his own image and likeness. He first formed the body of man which, though made of the slime of the earth, is the noblest work of visible creation. Into this body he breathed the breath of life. And man stood erect, a union of two substances: the one spiritual, the other material. Man, at his creation, was constituted by Almighty God in a state of grace and justice. The Lord placed Adam and Eve in a paradise of pleasure which he had planted from the beginning, and gave them rule over the fishes of the sea and the fowls of the air and all living creatures that move upon the earth (*Gen.* i. 26). And the Lord commanded man, saying: Of every tree of paradise thou shalt eat; but of the tree of knowledge of good and evil thou shalt not eat. For in what day soever thou shalt eat of it, thou shalt die the death (*Gen.* ii. 16, 17).

Eve, alas! yielded to the enticement of Satan, who had taken the form of a serpent; and along with Adam, Eve transgressed the commandment of Almighty God. Our first parents lost the friendship of the Lord by their disobedience. And the serpent, for having deceived the woman, was cursed by the Almighty, who said to it: I will put enmities between thee and the woman, and thy seed and her seed; she shall crush thy head. But who is she who is thus announced beforehand by the Lord as destined to coöperate in our redemption ? The Fathers with one voice respond that it is Mary. She, by giving birth to him who lives forever and ever, brought salvation to man, and introduced life into the world. Hail, fair daughter of Joachim ! Thou art she who, like the dawn announcing the approach of the sun, didst awaken the hopes of desponding mortals. By means of thee, the Savior of man appeared on the earth. Of thee it may be said that thou hast filled heaven, emptied hell, repaired the ruins of the celestial Jerusalem, and restored life to those who were lost in death (*St. Bernard*). Let us now prove that Mary may be said to have coöperated in our redemption because she gave her consent to the Incarnation of the Word, and because she had her part in the death of her Son.

I.

Scarcely had the first man fallen into sin when a sad and pernicious change took place, both in the moral and nat-

ural order.   Before the whole world
formed a delightful spectacle in the eyes
of Adam, and all creation contributed to
make him happy, even on earth. But
after the first sin a change came over all
things. The air grew dark and threatening.
The heavens showed their anger by thun-
der, hail, and tempests.   The earth trem-
bled, grew sterile, and required the sweat
of man before furnishing him with nour-
ishment.   The waters prepared their billows and whirlpools as instruments of
destruction. The seasons were disturbed;
and animals, forgetting their primitive
gentleness, became filled with fury
and thirsted after slaughter and blood.
Adam and Eve, despoiled of sanctity and
justice, for having violated the command
of God incurred the anger and indignation of the Lord, and consequently death,
with which they had before been threatened; and along with death, captivity
under the power of Satan, who thence-
forward held the empire of death. By
their sin they also suffered detriment in
body and in soul (*Con. Trid. Sess. 5, Can.* i).
Then commenced that fierce and endless
struggle between flesh and spirit mentioned by St. Paul (*Rom.*vii. 23).

But the God of mercy had written in
his eternal decrees, that man should have

a Redeemer: and as a woman was the occasion of all his misfortunes, he resolved that a woman should coöperate in his regeneration. He promised it himself in the beginning, and from time to time, through the patriarchs and prophets, he continued to indicate his design. Isaias raised his prophetic voice in the following words: There shall come a rod out of the root of Jesse, and a flower shall rise up out of his root. And the spirit of the Lord shall rest upon him (*Is.* ix. 1, 2). Behold, a virgin shall conceive and bear a son ; and his name shall be called Immanuel (*Is.* vii. 14). But who is this wonderful rod ? Who is this fortunate Virgin? It is Mary. Let us now examine carefully the evangelical history and learn in what manner she coöperated in the redemption of man.

The prophets of Israel were silent; the royal sceptre of Juda had passed to the hand of a stranger; the seventy weeks of Daniel were near their completion ; the whole world was in the enjoyment of profound peace, when all the creation was suddenly aroused by a brilliant light that burst forth from the highest heaven. It was the angel Gabriel, who, descending from heaven by order of God, presented himself to Mary in Nazareth, and said to her: Hail, full of grace; the Lord is with thee: Blessed art thou among women. And let not my unusual salutation cause thee to fear. I am a messenger of peace and I assure thee that thou hast found favor with God. He wishes to break the chains which hold man in the cruel slavery of sin; and he will make use of thee to present to the eyes of man his Lord and Savior. Behold, thou shalt conceive in thy womb and shalt bring forth a son; and thou shalt call his name Jesus. He shall be great and shall be called the son of the Most High; and the Lord God shall give unto him the throne of David, his father, and he shall reign in the house of Jacob forever (*Luke* i. 31, 32). Mary entertained no doubt of the fulfilment of the angel's declaration; but having made a vow of virginity she discreetly inquired in what manner it was to be accomplished. How shall this be done, for I know not man? The angel, answering, said to her, The Holy Ghost shall come upon thee, and the power of the Most High shall overshadow thee; and his work shall be the wonderful, immaculate, divine conception of Christ. And therefore also the Holy which shall be born of thee shall be called the Son of God. Heaven and earth awaited the answer of the Virgin of

Nazareth. St. Augustine and St. Bernard express, in a lively manner, the ardent desire of all intelligent beings, begging for the Incarnation of the Word, and supplicating Mary to yield her consent. The angel, O most blessed Virgin, stands in eager expectation of a favorable answer; and we, likewise, expect from thee the words of consolation and peace. We have all been condemned to death; but one word of thine will restore us to life. This, Adam, author of a ruined race,--this, Abraham, David, and all the Fathers of old, implore thee to utter. The whole world, prostrate at thy feet, entreats thy assent to the Incarnation. On thy lips depend the consolation of the miserable, the redemption of the captives, the salvation of all the children of Adam. Hasten to reply. Give joy to heaven and earth. Dismiss the angel with thy humble protestation of submission to the pleasure of God, that he may convey it to the eternal Word, now standing on the threshold of heaven ready to descend into thy bosom. When Mary's pure lips humbly pronounced the words--Behold the handmaid of the Lord: be it done to me according to thy word,--the union between the divine and human natures was consummated. The Word was made flesh; and the heavens and the earth resounded with a canticle of thanksgiving.

God, says William the Abbot, required the assent and coöperation of Mary, before operating in her the ineffable mystery of the Incarnation. He did not wish to take flesh from her unless she would freely grant it (*Cant.* ii.). The consent of the Virgin was one of the conditions of the Incarnation of the Word established in the eternal decrees of God ; and, according to St. Augustine, the word of Mary was to close or open heaven (*Serm.* xvii. *de Nat. Dom.*). The consent of Mary, expressed in the terms,—Be it done to me according to thy word, was the beginning of grace and salvation. Mary, by this reply, filled heaven with joy, supplied matter of exultation to all the angels, furnished hope to the world held captive, overwhelmed all the demons with terror, gladdened the celestial messenger, and promised deliverance to the Patriarchs and Prophets and all the ancient Fathers (*St. Laur. Giustin. Serm. de Annunt.*)

We also bear in mind that Mary not only assented to the Incarnation, but gave to the Divine Word the flesh which rendered him truly man and capable of satisfying for our sins by his bloody death, thus operating our redemption. The Blessed Virgin, says St. Antoninus (*P.* 4. *C.* 20), is to be considered, after God, under God, and with God, as an efficiènt cause of our redemption, because she gave her consent to the embassy of the Angel and gave birth to him who regenerated all men by his passion. She is to be regarded as a material cause also, because the Holy Ghost, with her approval, formed from the substance of her body the most sacred body of Jesus—that body by means of the tortures of which our redemption was completed, and men acquire once more the title of children of God. Albertus Magnus thus strongly expresses the share of the Blessed Virgin in our redemption : Whatever is cause of the cause, is cause of that which is produced by the cause ; but the Blessed Virgin is the cause of her Son, and her Son is the cause of all good and all mercy ; therefore his mother is also in her way the cause of all good and all mercy.

By sin man becomes guilty, and God is offended. To repair therefore the evils of sin, a being was required participating in the divine and human nature. It was necessary then that God should be concealed under human form. It was also settled in the eternal decrees that the second person of the adorable Trinity should offer an adequate compensation for the sins of men to the Divine Justice, by afflictions and torments. But how could the Word have accomplished this without human flesh? By the greatest of all miracles, the Word took in Mary and from Mary human substance and a body subject to suffering; and having united his human nature to the divine, in the Divine Person, was able to offer to his Father adequate satisfaction. We may therefore conclude with St. Thomas of Villanova (*Serm. de Assump.*): It is a dogma of our faith that Jesus Christ paid the price of our redemption. But it cannot be called in question, that Mary, by becoming his mother, furnished him with the means of satisfying the justice of God. He is our Redeemer, but from Mary he received the human substance in which he redeemed us. Mary is therefore not only the mother of God, but as mother of God, she coöperated in our redemption.

II.

We must reflect, in the second place, that, if written in the eternal decrees of God that the Divine Word should assume human nature for our redemption, this was not the limit of his humiliations.

The humiliations and torments of Christ were required—his sweat of blood, the blow on his cheek, the cruel scourge, the crown of thorns, the hatred of the rabble, the bearing of the cross, the nails through the Savior's hands and feet, the shedding of the last drop of his most precious blood, his agony and death upon the cross. To all the shame and sufferings of the Son and to his sacrifice on Calvary for the redemption of man, Mary gave her free and full consent.

In the opinion of the Fathers, Mary, by light derived from the Holy Ghost, comprehended more perfectly than the prophets themselves all that they had foretold concerning the Savior. The devout Rupertus (*in Cant. C.* 4) introduces Mary as speaking in the following manner: Souls restored to grace by my Son, and most dear to myself, do not confine your attention to that hour of anguish when I held in my arms the lifeless body of my Son; for the sword predicted by Simeon was continually transpiercing my heart. When I nourished him at my breast, I thought of the vinegar and gall which would be presented to him in his thirst; when I clothed him in his garments, I thought of the cords with which he would be bound; when I bore him in my arms,

I saw him hanging on the cross ; when he was tranquil in sleep, I saw him cold in death. All these trials and sorrows Mary freely and willingly accepted for the benefit of the human race.

Our redemption was accomplished by a sacrifice offered on the altar of the cross. This sacrifice was entirely consummated by Christ. He was at the same time priest and victim. Still Mary may be said to have part in it, for Christ, in offering himself to his Father, offered the flesh and blood which he had received from Mary (*St. Eucher. Hom.* i. *de Nativ. Dom.*). Mary loved God with perfect love ; in all things, therefore, her will was conformable to the will of God ; but it was the pleasure of God that his Son should undergo death on the cross for the salvation of man. Christ, therefore, and Mary, one in will, offered the same holocaust to the Almighty Father. On the summit of Golgotha, says Arnoldus Abbot, there were two altars—one in the body of Jesus, the other in the heart of Mary. And whilst Christ immolated himself in body, Mary sacrificed herself in heart. The writings of the Fathers abound with passages in which Mary's participation in the work of our redemption is depicted in the most lively colors, and exhibited as establishing a claim to our admiration, our veneration, and our warmest gratitude. Mary, then, did lend her coöperation in the accomplishment of man's redemption.

ASPIRATION.

Free us from our chains ; enlighten our eyes ; preserve us from evil ; obtain for us all that is needful.

PRACTICE.

Have instant recourse to Mary in time of trial, and bear up courageously in her honor.

LITANY.

Read Life of Blessed Virgin, by Abbé Orsini.

TWELFTH DAY.

THE LOVE WHICH WE OWE TO MARY.

"Thou art all fair, my love, and there is not a spot in thee." *Cant.* iv. 7.

THE spirit is filled with holy admiration, when we hear the spouse of the canticles addressing the Blessed Virgin in the

language applied to her by the Church :
Thou art all fair, O my love, and there is
not a spot in thee. Come from Libanus,
my spouse, come from Libanus, come;
thou shalt be crowned from the top of
Amana, from the top of Sanir and Her-
mon, from the dens of the lions, from the
mountains of the leopards. Thou hast
wounded my heart, my sister, my spouse
(*Cant.* iv. 7, 8, 9). Thy cheeks are as the
bark of a pomegranate (vi. 6). Thy stature
is like a palm tree, and thy eyes as those
of doves. Honey and milk are under thy
tongue, and the smell of thy garments as
the smell of frankincense (iv. 11). Thou
art all fair, O my love, and there is not a
spot in thee. Mary must have indeed been
adorned with celestial loveliness. The
Father chose her for his daughter, the
Son for his mother, and the Holy Ghost
for his spouse. On the day of her Assumption, the angels, dazzled by her beauty,
shouted with joy and exclaimed: Who
is she that cometh forth as the morning rising, fair as the moon, bright as
the sun (vi. 9) ? The Fathers of the
Church frequently represent Mary as
the dawn and the sun, and employ the
highest colorings of eloquence in setting
forth her dignity and her loveliness. If
Mary so charmed the heart of the Father

that he chose her for his daughter, and the heart of the Word that he destined her for his mother, and that of the Holy Ghost, that he wished her for his spouse ; if she excited wonder in the angels, and in every age made devout writers enthusiastic in the delineation of her magnificent qualities—we, in order to enkindle in our breasts a fervent and enduring love for Mary, may well devote our attention to the contemplation of her exterior and interior beauty.

I.

It is certain that God, in forming the human heart, inflamed it with affectionate feelings, in order that it might love him alone. But it frequently happens that, deluded by the charms of external appearances, or deceived by some rebellious passion representing evil for good, we devote our affections to follow display or the enticements of appetite, and thus bring ruin on our souls and outrage the majesty of Almighty God. We naturally love that which is presented to us as good: but God alone is essentially good; he is a vast ocean of all good; he contains in himself, in infinite perfection, whatever of good is distributed amongst his creatures. God alone therefore is worthy of all love. After God, Mary is first in goodness and beauty amongst all rational beings, all created things. God, in creating the world, made it a wonder of beauty and grandeur. He created the heavens and ornamented them with the sun, the moon and the stars. He created the earth and arranged in masterly order the mountains, the hills, the valleys, the seas, and the rivers. He formed the air and ordered the birds to flutter through it in their warblings. He peopled the deserts and forests with reptiles and animals of every kind. He beautified the hills with the peaceful olive and the odoriferous vine. He made the harvests wave yellow in the plains. He loaded the trees with exquisite fruits. He enamelled the prairies with flowers of every hue. He enlivened the waters of oceans, lakes, and rivers with fishes in countless variety. And all things he disposed in wonderful and harmonious order, that the world might become a delightful sojourn for man. But God, in creating Mary, formed her as a most especial world for himself. She was to be his dwelling place for nine months, and from her he took flesh and blood. Let who will, says Canisius, contemplate the harmony and beauty of the structure of the world, and admire what is most splendid and magnificent in the heavens and on the earth,—it all grows dim and disappears in the presence of Mary's glory.

The body of Christ, says Albertus Magnus, supernaturally formed by God himself, was most beautiful and most perfect, as beautiful and perfect as was consistent with the condition of a wayfarer on earth; in like manner the body of the Holy Virgin, designed for the human nature of Christ, was as beautiful and perfect as was consistent with her condition. If Christ was beautiful above the sons of men (*Ps.*xliv.3), then Mary was beautiful above all the daughters of Adam.

If Mary was beautiful by nature, because she was to become the tabernacle of the Most High, of the Holy of Holies, who can express the additional comeliness and splendor which she received from grace ? In the Blessed Virgin there was nothing either in body or soul that could blemish the splendor of her loveliness ; on the contrary, she was formed in body and soul according to the design of the sublime counsels of the Divine Wisdom. She was preserved from whatever could sully her beauty, and enriched with whatever could increase it.

The humanity of Christ, by reason of its personal union with the divine nature, was refulgent with every perfection of nature and grace; his mother, then, must have been in due proportion adorned with every perfection; for, after the hypostatic union, there can be no union more intimate than that between mother and son (*Dyon. Carth. lib.* i. *de Laud. V.*)

If we unfold the books of the old law, we meet in almost every page picturesque descriptions and charming images which shadow forth the splendor of the mother of God. Her beauty, interior and exterior, is prefigured by all that is most lovely in nature. It is mystically said of her, that she was exalted like a cedar in Libanus, and as a cypress tree on Mount Sion; that she was exalted like a palm tree in Cades, and as a rose plant in Jericho; as a fair olive tree in the plains, and as a plane tree by the water in the streets; that as the vine she brought forth a pleasant odor, and her flowers are the fruit of honor and riches (*Eccl.* xxiv.). She was also compared to the lily, to the rose, to sweet-smelling cinnamon, to the best myrrh, to the sun, and to the moon. The fragrance breathing from Mary, surpassing that of storax, and galbanum, and onyx, and aloes, and frankincense not cut, attracted the Maker of the universe, who determined that she should be the mother of the Son. Mary was most beautiful above all the illustrious women of the old law, although the highest praises are bestowed on their beauty. It was said of Judith that there was not such another woman upon earth in look, in beauty, and in sense of words (*Judith* xi. 19). Esther was exceedingly fair and beautiful (*Esther* ii. 7). Rebecca was an exceedingly comely maiden, a most beautiful virgin (*Gen.* xxiv. 16). Rachel was well favored and of a beautiful countenance (*Gen.* xxiv. 17). But Mary excelled them all in beauty and loveliness. God himself, as the Church understands it, celebrates in the Canticles the praises of Mary. Who is she that goeth up by the desert, as a pillar of smoke of aromatical spices, of myrrh and frankincense, and of all the powders of the perfumer (*Cant.* iii. 6) ? Thou art beautiful, O my love, sweet and comely as Jerusalem (vi. 3). My dove in the clifts of the rock, in the hollow places of the wall, show me thy face ; let thy voice sound in my ears, for thy voice is sweet and thy face comely (ii. 14). Turn away thy face from me ; for they have made me flee away (vi. 4). The daughters saw thee, and declared thee most blessed ; the queens, and they praised thee (vi. 8).

We learn from St. Paul that when we shall become citizens of heaven Jesus Christ will reform the body of our lowness, made like to the body of his glory, according to the operation whereby also he is able to subdue all things unto himself (*Philip.*iii. 21). Glory then will be one of the properties of the bodies of the blessed after the general resurrection. But as there is one glory of the sun, another glory of the moon, and another glory of the stars,—for star differeth from star in glory,—so also is the resurrection of the dead (1 *Cor.* xv. 41, 42). The glory, therefore, of the saints in heaven will be different, not in soul only, but also in body. This difference will be determined by the inequality of the merits acquired on earth. As the soul of the Blessed Virgin enjoys in heaven an unspeakable glory responding to her merits on earth, how passing great must be the splendor, the glory, of her external appearance !

St. Augustine and St. Bernard teach that the beauty of the Blessed Virgin was shown in figure to St. John, the evangelist, when he saw that sublime queen crowned with twelve stars, having the moon under her feet, and arrayed in robes of magnificence formed of the rays of the sun (*Apoc.* xii. 1). As there is no light on earth to be compared with that of the sun, the moon and the stars, so there is no beauty in heaven, either in saints or angels, to be compared with the beauty of the Holy Virgin Mary. In her presence all other created beauty fades and disappears. God alone is beauty in essence, and from him descend all the beauty and grace which are found in all rational and angelic beings. All created beauty may be said to be a mere participation of the beauty of Almighty God. According to St. Thomas (*III. P.* 9, 27), the nearer anything approaches its principle the more it partakes of the effect of the principle; but Mary is more closely allied with God than all saints and angels because she is the mother of God; therefore she draws more copiously from the source of all beauty and loveliness than saints and angels all united.   The saints are fair in the sight of heaven; but how much fairer is Mary ! The angels and archangels are clothed with fairness; but if we pass in review all the celestial choirs in their increasing degrees of beauty, we are forced to ex-

claim, as each one moves before us,
More lovely far is Mary!   Let us, then,
chant with the Church, The holy mother
of God is exalted above all the choirs of
angels in the heavenly kingdom.

II.

When our admiration is attracted by
an edifice, which, in all its external parts,
is a miracle of architectural skill, we are
naturally led to suppose that the interior is glittering with art, elegance, and
wealth.   In like manner, when we contemplate the loveliness which adorned
Mary on earth, and the external glory
which surrounds her in heaven, we in-
stinctively turn our thoughts to the
beauty of her soul.   But all the glory of
the king's daughter is within (*Ps.* xliv.
14).   The most brilliant charms of Mary
are therefore concealed from external
view.

. Mary was enriched with a plenitude
of all the treasures of grace, and thus
made so acceptable in the eyes of God,
that she was chosen to be his mother.
Albertus Magnus avers that the Blessed
Virgin possessed in the highest degree
all general and special graces granted to
all creatures ; that she was replenished

with grace in such copiousness that
it was not imparted more abundantly
to any created being. For she contained
within, God, who is grace increate. According to Suarez, the Blessed Virgin, from the first instant of her conception and sanctification, was loved more
by the Divine Word than all angels and
men. For from that instant he loved
her as his future mother; and as the grace
communicated corresponds to the love
entertained, he bestowed more abundant
grace upon her who was to be his mother
than upon all the saints and angels together. Mary, says St. Bernardine, had in
an eminent manner her abode in the full
assembly of saints. For she was dignified with the faith of the patriarchs, the
inspiration of the prophets, the zeal of
the apostles, the constancy of the martyrs, the sanctity of the confessors, the
chastity of the virgins, the fruitfulness of
the wedded, the purity of the angels
(*St. Bern. in Verb. Eccl.* xxiv. 16). How
great must be the splendor of the glory
of Mary's soul in heaven ! St. Bernardine
teaches that the glory of the Blessed Virgin is as different from the glory of the
other blessed as the sun is different from
the other celestial luminaries; and as the
other celestial bodies are regulated by

the sun, so the whole heavenly court is ornamented and rejoiced by the glorious Virgin Mary. The source of all this glory is the divine maternity of Mary. If Mary was supremely fair in body and in soul, if she was full of grace on earth, and in heaven is supereminently resplendent in glory, she is the greatest and most lovely of all pure creatures, and deserves that we should love her with the fondest affection.

ASPIRATION.

From all sin deliver us, Holy Virgin Mary.

PRACTICE.

Think frequently of the greatness of Mary.

LITANY.

Read Reflections on the Litany of Loretto.

THIRTEENTH DAY.

HOW TO STUDY MARY, THE MOTHER OF GRACE.

"Arise, O Lord, into thy resting place, thou and the ark which thou hast sanctified." *Ps.* cxxi. 8.

THE creator of all things, a most pure spirit, majesty and holiness itself, when he determined to dwell with the Hebrews in the desert, commanded a tabernacle to be constructed for his especial abode, whence he would deliver his oracles. But listen with what grandeur of art he required it to be constructed and with what costliness he adorned it. Frame an ark of setim wood, he said to Moses, and thou shalt overlay it with the purest gold within and without; and over it thou shalt make a golden crown round about, and four golden rings, which thou shalt put at the four corners of the ark. Thou shalt make bars also of setim wood, and shalt overlay them with gold. And thou shalt put them in through the rings in the sides of the ark, that it may be carried on them. Thou shalt make also a propitiatory of the finest gold as a covering for the ark. Thou shalt make also two cherubim of beaten gold on the two sides of the oracle. Let one cherub be on the one side, and the other on the other. Let them cover both sides of the propitiatory, spreading their wings, and covering the oracle, and let them look one towards the other, their faces being turned towards the propitiatory. Thence will I give orders, and will speak to thee over the propitiatory, and from the midst of the two cherubim, which shall be upon the ark of the testimony, all things which I will command the children of Israel by thee (*Exod.* xxv.). St. Bernard says (*de B. V. Deip.* ii. 9), that the ark of the testimony was a figure of the most holy mother of God. As the ark of the testimony, besides being formed of gold and precious wood, contained the objects most holy to the Hebrews, so Mary, besides being the most beautiful creature in Nature, was also the most holy creature of grace; for the Almighty lavished all the graces upon her and resided in her as a king in his kingdom, a father in the dwelling place of his family, a pontiff in the temple, a spouse in the room of his spouse. The Most High created her expressly for himself, and adorned her with justice, sanctity and every grace, so that she addressed her servants in the words of Divine Wisdom—I am the mother of fair love, and of fear, and of knowledge, and of holy hope. In me is all grace of the way and of the truth ; in me is all hope of life and of virtue. Come over to me, all ye that desire me, and be filled with my fruits (*Eccl.* xxiv. 24). For my fruit is better than gold, and the precious stone, and my blossoms better than choice silver. He that shall find me shall find life and shall have salvation from the Lord (*Prov.* viii. 10, 35). Let us now examine the reasons for which Mary is called the Mother of Grace, and brings grace to those who devoutly honor her.

I.

The name of Mother of Grace is a name pleasant and dear to all the servants of Mary; and the countenance of infancy and old age, when they repeat it, is brightened with a smile of holy joy. The name of Mother of Grace is a name of glory, which points out her who from all eternity was the object of the predilection of God above all other creatures, and was enriched by him with the fullness of all graces and benedictions. The title of Mother of Grace is a title of beneficence, for it awakens the recollection of favors received from Mary, by which the multiplied hardships of earthly exile are alleviated, and recalls to mind the graces received from Almighty God through her mediation for the persuit and attainment of a blessed immortality. When did Mary obtain the fullness of grace from which arises her title of Mother of Grace? In her conception, at her birth, and at the time when the angel announced to her that she was to be the Mother of God.

In the doctrine of St. Thomas, Almighty God distributes his graces to his saints with a view to the dignity and office to which he destines them : the Blessed Virgin, destined to be the mother of the Word incarnate and queen of all the saints, must have received the fullness of grace at the very instant of her immaculate conception. According to theologians, Mary enjoyed three privileges not shared by the other mere creatures. Her wonderful holiness was original, inamissible, and always increasing. The first man and the angels were constituted in sanctifying grace, but with the power of forfeiting it, as man and many angels did ; but Mary in her conception was filled with holiness which she never forfeited, and, by especial privilege could not lose. The apostles were confirmed in grace after the descent of the Holy Ghost, still they were not exempt from slight defects; but Mary, from the first moment of her existence, was unchangeably united with God, and was made by grace incapable of sinning. The blessed in heaven are free from every moral imperfection, and enjoy a sanctity that can suffer no change and admit no blemish; but their holiness receives no increase, whilst the holiness of Mary grew greater every day as long as she remained on earth. The grace bestowed on Mary the first instant of her conception was augmented to the highest degree of perfection by the gifts of the Holy Ghost, the infused habits of the moral and intellectual virtues, the gift of prophecy, of miracles, and of the understanding of the Scriptures. Why mention the use of free will granted to her by Almighty power before the natural time (*St. Bernardinus*)? Why the privilege, properly belonging to the angels, of thinking and contemplating in a manner altogether spiritual and without dependence on the senses? Although the imagination of Mary was as yet in a kind of bondage, and the organs of her body were as yet unfit for the full exercise of their functions, the soul of Mary was not inactive. The mist which darkens the minds of other children imprisoned in the bosom of their mothers, did not extinguish the light of her spirit. The heart watched, and operating with God, overflowed with delights; so that the time before birth, which in others passes away unproductive, was in Mary a time of benediction and merit.

Mary was enriched with every grace at the time of her birth. She was free from sin and the effects of sin, and had no experience in her own person of that fatal law of the members contrary to the law of God, through which every man, however just, groans under the weight of the flesh in constant rebellion against the spirit. She was not exposed to those combats in which man at one time conquers, at another is conquered; but she lived in a delightful peace that was never disturbed by the agitation of unruly inclinations. The propensity to evil, which is born with us, and harasses us to the last hour of life, never had existence in Mary. By the operation of grace she seemed to be of a nature different from ours, being exempt from our infirmities, sovereign mistress of all the affections of her soul, freed from the slavery of the children of Adam, and ever walking before God in perfect innocence of heart. All the degrees of greatness in Mary had their beginning in her conception, as the seed of the tree contains in a certain way all the excellence and beauty of the fruit. The Blessed Virgin entered the world as a sovereign; all others enter it as slaves. She came as Queen of the Angels, because by means of her the seats were to be occupied which had been rendered vacant by the rebellion of the evil spirits. She came as Queen of the Patriarchs and Prophets,because through her the oracles of God had their fulfilment. She came as Queen of the Apostles, because her birth gave commencement to the gospel which they were to preach. She came as Queen of the Virgins and of all the Saints, because she was born in the state of grace, and in the plenitude of innocence.

But if we reflect more attentively in what circumstance the Blessed Virgin was full of the Holy Ghost, and of all his gifts of grace, we shall discover that it was at the moment of her annunciation, when she became the mother of the Eternal Word. Hail, said the angel to Mary on the part of God, Hail, full of grace, for the Lord dwells with thee, and thou art blessed with every blessing, above all the women of all ages. Fear not illusion or deception, for thou hast found grace before God. Thou shalt conceive and bring forth the Redeemer of the world, and thou shalt call his name Jesus. Unsullied thy virginity shall remain ; for the Holy Ghost shall come upon thee, and the power of the Most High shall overshadow thee (*Luke* i. 38). We learn here from the Gospel that Mary, being a virgin, became a mother without prejudice to her virginal honor, and that she became the mother of the Son of God. That a virgin should become a mother, and the mother of God, is a miracle so great that a greater cannot have place in the eternal operations of the Almighty (*St. Bernardine, Serm.* 61: *St. Aug. Epist.* 3 *ad Volus*). Of the only-begotten Son of God the Virgin Mary is mother; a worthy mother of a worthy son, an immaculate mother of a holy son ; a unique mother of a unique son. No other only-begotten can come upon the earth ; and no other virgin can be mother of the only-begotten (*Orig. Serm.* 2). No other creature can contract so strict an affinity with God as the Blessed Virgin, because the mother and the son have the same flesh—one common substance. The flesh of Christ, says St. Augustine (*Serm. de B. V. M.*), is the flesh of Mary. As long as a son, says St. Thomas, is in the bosom of his mother, he is not separated from her, but forms a part of her by a tie of nature, as the fruit hanging from the tree is reputed a part of the tree itself. No more intimate union after the hypostatic can be conceived than that of Mary with her son. By this union she approached the confines of Divinity. The three persons of the most Holy Trinity, says St. Bernard (*Serm. de B. M. Deip.*), concurred to enrich Mary with their gifts and treasures. The Father imparted to her the power to become a mother, the Son wisdom to enlighten her, the Holy Ghost the grace of all virtues. The Father conferred upon her the authority against sin, the Son humility against the world, the Holy Ghost charity towards God and the neighbor. The Father gave to Mary the contemplation of heavenly things, the Son instructed her to operate virtuously, the Holy Ghost raised her to heaven on the wings of faith. The three persons of the most Holy Trinity, to express much in few words, bestowed upon Mary the purity of the angels, the charity of the apostles, the fortitude of the martyrs, the sanctity of the confessors, the wisdom of the doctors, the abstinence of the anchorites, the modesty of the religious, the devotion of the priests, the integrity of the virgins, the continence of the widows, and the fruitfulness of the wedded. Mary, therefore, is mother of grace, because she is mother of the Author of Grace, because she was pleasing to God in the exercise of every virtue ; and because she received in superabundance, above angels and saints, the plenitude of all graces.

II.

The Angelic Doctor teaches us that another species of fulness of grace is found in Mary, which is an advantage to all men, and especially of encouragement to sinners and consolation to the afflicted. We wonder, he says (*Op.* 8), that in each saint there is grace sufficient for the salvation of many, but our wonder is exceedingly great when we reflect that there is in Christ and in the Virgin grace sufficient for the salvation of all men. God, being about to rescue the human race from the slavery of Satan and sin, committed the whole price of redemption to Mary. She, according to the Fathers, furnished the beginning of salvation and grace, and is to be considered as a cause of salvation for having conceived the Author of grace and given a Redeemer to the world (*St. Bernardine*). The Lord was with Mary, and Mary was with the Lord, coöperating in the same labor and in the same work

of redemption. (*St. Bernardine, ibid* i. 1).
We see Mary at the manger, at the temple,
in Egypt, in Galilee, in Jerusalem, in the
solitudes, in the deserts, always with Jesus.
On that last day of anguish and sorrow,
when the redemption of the human race
was completed at the price of infinite torture, Mary followed faithfully the footsteps
of her Son ; and when he hung in agony
between heaven and earth, she stood in agony at the foot of the cross. Every affliction of her Son waked a corresponding affliction in her motherly heart. There were
two altars on Golgotha, the one in the heart
of Mary, the other in the body of Jesus.
Jesus immolated his flesh, Mary her soul, for
the benefit of sinners. Jesus, seeing the
sacrifice of love which Mary was offering
in our behalf, although on the point of
breathing forth his soul, arouses himself,
and says to John: Beloved disciple, dost
thou see the affliction of my mother ? For
thee also she suffers ; take her as a mother;
as such I give her to thee (*John* xix. 27).

If Mary conceived and gave birth to
the Author of grace ; if she coöperated in
the work of our redemption ; if she was
replenished with all graces for the benefit of men ; if she was given to us as a
mother by the Redeemer himself on Calvary ; shall we not esteem her as a mother

who is the bearer of grace to her children? From the gospel it is evident that she is such a mother. Jesus and Mary were present at the marriage in Galilee. Mary perceived that the wine had failed, and compassionating the confusion of the spouses, she said to Jesus, They have no wine. And Jesus saith to her, Woman, what is that to me and thee? My hour is not yet come (*John ii.* 34.). Notwithstanding this reply, the application of Mary proved successful, and Jesus changed water to wine to supply the deficiency. The first miracle of Jesus Christ was performed at the intercession of his mother. This shows what confidence we should repose in the kindness of our good mother. The Eternal Father wills that through her we should receive every good thing, since he willed that through her we should receive his only-begotten Son, in whom he has given us all things. The loving zeal of this mother in favor of her children was prefigured in the history of Esther. Assuerus, inflamed with anger against the Hebrews, had signed the decree of extermination, commanding that all the Hebrews in his kingdom should be put to death on the same day—men and women, old and young. But Esther, who before had found favor before the king, and had been crowned his queen, changed by her entreaties the heart of Assuerus, and prevailed upon him to recall the fatal decree. Mary exerts herself in the same manner in our behalf, and our sorrow is turned into joy. Her kindness toward the sorrowing was great whilst she was in her pilgrimage on earth, but far greater is it now that she is reigning in heaven. Knowing our miseries better now, she obtains grace for us more abundantly. As the brilliancy of the sun exceeds that of the moon, so the compassion of Mary exceeds the compassion which she felt for us on earth. And as the sun sends down its rays upon wealthy and needy, Mary showers down her favors upon just men and sinners—upon the just to justify them still, and upon the sinners to enlighten them to the life of grace. Who could enumerate the graces bestowed by the mother of grace? As the raindrops which descend to refresh and fertilize the earth are beyond the power of enumeration, so countless are the graces which Mary causes to descend upon the children of men. This is testified by the multitudes who hurry to her sanctuaries, the votive tablets that hang around her altars, the lights that are always burning before her images.

ASPIRATION.

Mary, Mother of Grace, Mother of Mercy, defend us from our enemies, and receive us at the hour of death.

PRACTICE.

Perform some spiritual or corporal work of mercy in honor of the Blessed Virgin.

LITANY.

Read Mary, Star of the Sea.

FOURTEENTH DAY.

THE VIRGINITY OF MARY.

"The Lord appeared to him in a flame of fire out of the midst of a bush ; and he saw that the bush was on fire, and was not burnt." *Exod.*iii. 2.

THE Hebrews were groaning under a most cruel slavery in the land of Egypt, and Moses, disregarding the riches of the Pharaos, chose rather to suffer persecution with the people of God, esteeming the approach of Christ greater riches than the treasure of the Egyptians (*Heb.*

ix. 25). Reduced to poverty, slighted, and suspected, not only by the Egyptians, but by his own brethren, he fled secretly into the arid deserts of Arabia, and finally fixed his abode in the land of Madian. There he awaited with resignation the interference of Divine Mercy in favor of the Hebrews, and employed himself in tending the flocks of Jethro, his father-in-law. Having conducted the flocks into the interior of the desert and arrived at the mountain of God, Horeb, he witnessed an extraordinary spectacle. He beheld at a distance a bush enveloped in flames, and still no portion of it was consumed. When he went forward to see why the bush was not burnt, he heard the voice of the Lord, who said to him: Come not nigh hither ; put off the shoes from thy feet ; for the place whereon thou standest is holy ground (*Exod.* iii. 8). He afterwards disclosed to him his intention of delivering his people from the tyranny of the Egyptians ; and informed him that he was to be the instrument by means of which their deliverance was to be accomplished. But the bush that burned without being consumed, what hidden signification has it, and of what was it a symbol ? The Church recognizes in that burning bush the praiseworthy virginity of Mary. (*in Off. Purif.*). And virginity is indeed commendable, and to be extolled to the skies with praises, for it is written in the Apocalypse that virgins have a separate place assigned to them before the throne of the lamb. Why do we call Mary the Queen of the Virgins? The development of the reasons will increase our devotion for her, and excite us to love so fair a virtue.

I.

Virginal purity is a moral virtue which rejects every species of carnal delight. This divine virtue possesses charms so powerful that God leaves heaven for earth to converse with virgins, the inseparable companions of the Lamb, the most illustrious portion of the flock of the Lord, and the richest treasure of the Church. The innocent soul is a worthy temple of God on earth, and with its virginal purity it holds secure the gifts of grace and of the Holy Ghost. Grace always present removes all alluring thoughts which might give food to concupiscence and not only prevents the slightest glimmering of this infernal fire from reaching the will, but diligently watches over the appetite itself. The excellence of the virtue of virginity is such, that nothing else causes

either soul or body to approach so
nearly that state of felicity to which we
shall be exalted, that life which, after the
general resurrection, we shall lead in
heaven, rescued from death, not subject
to corruption, incorruptible and immortal. This felicity appears to be indicated
by Christ when he says that in the resurrection they shall neither marry nor be
given in marriage, but shall be as the
angels of God in heaven (*Matt.* xxii. 30).
He, therefore, who remains in a state of
celibacy, and preserves his heart immaculate by purity of mind and body, makes
the nearest approach in his life on earth
to the life of glory in heaven. St. Basil
affirms that virginity renders man similar
to the incorruptible God (*Lib. de Virg.*).

Mary holds the first place in virginity,
not only amongst men, but even amongst
angels. Hence she is saluted by the
Church as Mother most pure, Queen of
Virgins. The virginal purity of Mary excels in perfection that of the angels, because they possess it by nature, Mary by
grace. In the angels it is of necessity,
in Mary it proceeds from free will. The
angels preserve it in a nature inaccessible
to concupiscence, Mary in a nature surrounded by frailty. Mary far surpasses
in virginity all creatures of a nature in-

ferior to the angels, because the resolution to preserve it intact was in her more firm, more noble, more perfect. Mary was ennobled with all the graces of the patriarchs, the prophets, the apostles, the martyrs, the confessors, the virgins, and all the other saints; she is like the sea, that gathers into its bosom all the waters of the rivers; she was able, consequently, to form more perfect acts of love of God. Her virginity, therefore, excelled in perfection the virginity of all the saints. Mary confirmed her resolution to observe virginity by a perpetual vow, and was free from concupiscence, which so fiercely opposes its observance. She not only never experienced the rebellion of nature, but breathed around such a fragrance of innocence, that all who approached her were inflamed with love of purity. Her resolution was therefore more firm and efficacious than the resolution of all others. It was more noble too, because it prepared her for the dignity of Mother of God.

Mary is Queen of Virgins. Her virginity then, must be embellished with qualities altogether new to the world. What more unheard of than virginity and motherhood united in the same person! What more new than that a most pure

Virgin, not knowing man, should give birth to a son! That a Virgin should become a mother by the operation of the Holy Ghost! That a virgin, free from what is common to all other mothers, should. become the mother of God! The decisions of councils in this point (*Later. Sub. Mart. V. Roman, an.* 389. *Mediolan. Nicaen. etc.*), the doctrine of the Church, the teaching of the Fathers and the Divines, are familiar to every Catholic. All proclaim that Mary was a virgin when she conceived, a virgin when she brought forth her son, a virgin forever after (*St. Aug. de Cat. Rud. c.* 22). The Church chants the praises of Mary as a virgin in a manner altogether peculiar and unknown to other virgins—Virgo singularis. And does not she alone wear the diadem of the mother of the King of kings, by which she claims dominion over angels and saints? Did either nature or grace ever produce a virgin like Mary? Mary is most holy amongst the holy, most pure amongst the pure, a celestial wonder, the mirror of virtues, the miracle of the world, the joy of heaven and earth. She alone is virgin and mother; virgin without example and without equal; mother of the author of grace. She is virgin in body, in mind, in look, in thought, in feel-

ings, in word, and in work. As the eagle
soars above all the feathered tribe, the
Virgin Mary soars above all other virgins. Almighty God himself, in various
parts of scriptures, has exhibited under
beautiful images the singular excellence
of the virginity of Mary. She is the virgin
rose that opens its purple-tinted bosom to
the kindly influence of the heavenly dew ;
she is the lily amongst thorns that diffuses
around an aroma of fragrance; she is the
fair and innocent dove that reflects all the
various colors of light in presence of the
sun ; she is the immortal palm, the incorruptible cedar, the triumphant laurel, the
turpentine tree with spreading branches
and dense foliage. Of her were figures,
the terrestrial paradise, the tree of life,
the well enclosed garden, the sealed fountain, the mirror without blemish, the
ark of Noe and of the covenant, the little
cloud seen by Elias, the fleece of Gideon,
the tabernacle and the temple. She was
the closed gate through which was to
pass, without its being opened, the God
made man, the consoler of the afflicted,
the hope of Israel, the Savior of the
human race, the desire of all just souls; he
was to throw open the gates of heaven
closed by sin, and to fill with souls redeemed by himself the seats left vacant

by the rebellion of Lucifer. These and numberless others were the symbols which foreshadowed that illustrious maiden, who was chosen to be the mother of God without suffering the slightest detriment to her virginal purity.

Besides the symbols, there are innumerable passages in scripture which allude to the virginity of Mary. Isaias clearly foretells that the Savior should be born of a virgin. Behold a virgin shall conceive and shall bear a son, and his name shall be called Emmanual (*Is.* vii. 14). Again he said, There shall come forth a rod out of the root of Jesse, and a flower shall rise up out of his root. And the spirit of the Lord shall rest upon him (*Is.* xi. 1, 2). The land that was desolate and impassable shall be glad; the wilderness shall rejoice, and flourish like the lily. It shall bud forth and blossom, and shall rejoice with joy and praise; the glory of Libanus is given to it; the beauty of Carmel and Saron : they shall see the glory of the Lord, and the beauty of our God (*Is.* xxxv. 1, 2). But whilst he described the blessings of redemption, he foreknew that Christ would be born of a virgin mother; and the honor of the son redounds to the honor of the mother.

When the beauty of a flower is admired, the stem which produced it is praised; when the fruits of a tree are carefully watched and gathered, by the very act the good qualities of the tree itself, and the seed from which it arose, are commended. God, moreover, in the mystic explanation of the Church, called her all fair, and without stain of sin to tarnish her virginal innocence. Thou art all fair, O my love, and there is no spot in thee (*Cant.* iv. 6). Fair as the moon, bright as the sun (*Cant.* vi. 9). As there is no heavenly body more beautiful than the sun and the moon, so there is no creature more passing fair than the spotless Virgin Mary.   .

II.

But the claims of Mary to the title of Queen of Virgins are not yet exhausted. She consecrated her body to God by a vow of perpetual virginity. This is the opinion of St. Augustine, St. Bernard, St. Ildefonsus, and all the doctors of the Church. The holy virgin was not ignorant that herself and all other creatures belonged entirely to God, because from him they derived their being; and she wished to consecrate herself solemnly to him in the presence of angels and men, on the day of her presentation in the temple, when she was only three years of age. This resolution was inspired by the holy Ghost, and she executed it with all the devotion and fervor of her soul. She loved God with her whole heart and her whole strength, and her only thought was to give him pleasure. She knew also that the merit of virginity is increased by the obligation of a vow to maintain it; and she chose the part which was more perfect, more secure, and more glorious to the Lord. Then were verified in her the words of the Holy Ghost, by whom she was already regarded as a spouse:—My sister, my spouse, is a garden enclosed, a fountain sealed up (*Cant.* iv. 12). The Holy Spirit repeated twice the words, " a garden enclosed," because she was equally pure in body and soul; and to place her virginity in security, she reared around it, by means of a perpetual vow, a powerful barrier, in order to break all the assaults of the unclean spirit of the abyss; and she strengthened this defence by intrusting it to the guardianship of humility, modesty, silence, and temperance. St. Augustine, and after him the Fathers and theologians, wishing to prove that the Blessed Virgin had consecrated her virginity to God by vow, bring forward her words to the angel, when he announced to her that she should be the mother of the Word Incarnate. How shall this be done, because I know not man (*Luke* i. 34)? Mary by these words did not express a doubt that the mystery foretold by the angel would have its accomplishment; she wished merely to be informed of the manner in which it was to be accomplished, bearing in mind the vow of perpetual virginity which she had made from her earliest days. Her question to the angel is an evident proof that she had dedicated herself to God in soul and in body. If she was espoused to Joseph this was not for the loss, but for the protection, of her virginity.

Some, perhaps, before Mary, had the will to preserve the fair virtue of virginity, as Elias, Eliseus, Jeremias, and Daniel; but before her no one consecrated it to God, and bound the will forever by a perpetual vow. Under the old covenant a vow of virginity, or rather sterility, a necessary consequence of it, was viewed as a reproach, a disgrace, and a curse to a family (*Ex.* xxiii. 36). When Rachel gave birth to Joseph, she exclaimed, God hath taken away my reproach (*Gen.* xxx. 23)! When the daughter of Jepthe learned from her father that she was to be offered in sacrifice, in fulfilment of a vow which he had made to the Lord, she said to him; My Father, if thou hast opened thy mouth to the Lord, do unto me whatsoever thou hast promised. Grant me only this which I desire: Let me go, that I may go about the mountains, and may bewail my virginity with my companions (*Judges* xi. 36). Besides the disgrace of celibacy, the desire of giving birth to the Savior of the world had seized upon the hearts of all Hebrew maidens. In the new testament as soon as Mary unfolded the snow-white standard of virginity, innumerable bands of virgins immediately rallied around her. In the first bloom of their age they consecrated their hearts to God, and under the triumphant banner of the Virgin, courageously and successfully combated against the devil and the flesh. Thus were fulfilled the words of the prophet when he sang to the sound of his golden harp. After her shall virgins be brought to the king; her neighbors shall be brought to thee. They shall be brought into the temple of the King (*Ps.* xliv. 14). Mary is therefore Queen of Virgins, because she was the first to bind herself by perpetual vow to maintain unsullied the fair and angelic virtue of virginity.

ASPIRATION.

From the spirit of uncleanness, deliver us, O Virgin Mary.

PRACTICE.

Keep a strict watch over all your senses, especially your eyes.

LITANY.

Consult Angelus Domini, illustrated in Art.

FIFTEENTH DAY.

MARY, MOTHER OF CHASTITY.

"This gate shall be shut; it shall not be opened; and no man shall pass through it; because the Lord the God of Israel hath entered by it." *Ezech.* xliv. 2.

WHILST Jeremias was in Jerusalem Ezechiel was in Babylon; and both spoke with prophetic spirit and made manifest the designs of God. Ezechiel in the land of his exile often wandered along the banks of the river Chobar, as being a place of silence and retirement and well suited for religious meditation.

There God revealed to him the chastisement with which he intended to visit the wickedness of the Hebrews, the destruction of Jerusalem and of the temple, the punishments which he designed to inflict upon the nations bordering upon Judea, upon the Chaldeans themselves and the haughty Babylon. He revealed to him also the happy return of the Hebrews to their country, the restoration of Jerusalem and of the temple, and the new alliance which he would contract with his repentant people. In a vision Ezechiel was conveyed in spirit to Jerusalem, and God by means of an angel showed him the measurements and the design of the grand fabric of the new temple. He pointed out to him, as if it were already built, the exterior gate of the sanctuary turned towards the east; it was closed, and Ezechiel saw the glory of the God of Israel enter by it, and the Lord said to him: This gate shall be shut; it shall not be opened; and no man shall pass through it, because the Lord the God of Israel hath entered by it. The Fathers of the Church and all Catholic interpreters recognize in that gate a beautiful figure of the Blessed Virgin, in whose bosom the Divine Word took upon himself human nature without impairing her virginity either in his conception or in his birth. What signifies, says St. Augustine, the closed door in the house of the Lord, if not that Mary shall remain always inviolate? What signify those words, And no man shall pass through it, if not the purity of Joseph? Of what is it a symbol that God alone passes through it, if not of the divine conception operated by the power of the Holy Ghost? What means it that this gate shall be closed forever, if not that Mary was a virgin before she gave birth to her Son, a virgin when she gave birth to him, and a virgin ever after? (*Serm. de Nat. Dom.*) It is easy now to understand that Mary is Mother of Chastity. Let us now consider more attentively the peculiar excellence of the chastity of Mary.

I.

Chastity is a most sublime virtue, by which both soul and body are preserved pure and unsullied. According to the Angelic Doctor (2. 2. 9. 151. a. 1.), the virtue of chastity derives its name from the Latin word *castigare*, to chastise; because by it the concupiscence of the flesh is chastised and curbed in order to subject it to the yoke of reason. We attribute to Mary the denomination of most chaste, because she was free from the passion contrary to chastity, and because she maintained her purity in its fullest integrity above every other creature.

Every object that we meet with in this world hurries us along to sin and perdition; but what we have most to fear is the implacable enemy that lies concealed within ourselves, like the treacherous serpent which hides itself under the herbage in order to strike the heel of the unguarded traveler. St. Paul, the apostle, speaking from experience, thus complains: I see another law in my members, fighting against the law of my mind, and captivating me in the law of sin that is in my members. Unhappy man that I am! Who shall deliver me from the body of this death ? The grace of God by Jesus Christ our Lord (*Rom.* vii. 26). These expressions prove clearly that the great apostle, although called to the apostleship by the most extraordinary grace, was subject to the severest assaults of sense, and that his soul was tormented by rebellious concupiscence. Human nature in the first man, having fallen and been vitiated by sin, the penalty of this sin descended to all men; so that nature itself, which was created good and upright by Almighty God, is taken for the fault and infirmity of corrupt nature, because its inclinations, if left to themselves, lead to evil and the things of earth. For that small portion of power which remained in nature is as a spark concealed beneath the ashes (*Im. Christi* 1, 3; *c.* 41). Our body produces briers and thorns; hence so many stings of temptation, and goadings of foul imaginations, which assail and frequently ruin chastity. But the Virgin, the most blessed mother of God, was exempt from every incitement to sin, from every inclination contrary to reason. She never felt in her heart, as we do, the tumultuous whirlpool of numerous passions producing blindness by their wild commotion. She never experienced the law of the flesh, so contrary to the law of the Spirit. Preserved from original sin, she was free from its effects and was undisturbed by concupiscence, so destructive to the soul of man. The Lord dwelt in the heart of Mary, and his place was in peace (*Ps.* lxxv. 2).

Mary, however, during her whole life, employed the most active vigilance in guarding the inestimable treasure which she possessed. Although unknown to the infirmities of corrupt nature, she maintained as much watchfulness as if in everything and everywhere she had

had something to fear, something to dread. When a child of three years, she retired to the temple and was reared within its sacred precincts; she grew up in the exercise of the most eminent virtues; she lived apart from the world in silence and solitude; she was an utter stranger to the vanity, the luxury, the pomps and pleasures, which charm and enslave the hearts of the worldly minded. And she thus left a memorable example in condemnation of those who heedlessly expose the treasure of purity to so many manifest dangers. Mary, moreover, to keep farther from herself every enemy of the purity of her heart, cultivated assiduously the virtues of humility, modesty, temperance, diligence, silence, and devout contemplation—fair and august daughters of heaven; and they shielded her against all those forces which the world, the flesh, and the spirits of darkness marshal in battle to overwhelm our virtue. St. Ambrose very well says of Mary, that she was a virgin not only in body but in mind; that she was humble in heart, grave in words, prudent in spirit, little inclined to speak, diligent in persuing the Holy Scriptures and in avoiding every danger that she might devote herself wholly to God.

But the most excellent and singular prerogative of the chastity of Mary was, that she not only never experienced the rebellion of concupiscence, but inspired all who beheld her with love for angelic purity. So great was the grace of the Virgin, says St. Ambrose (*de Instit. Virg.*), that she not only maintained her own purity in all its matchless dignity, but infused into those who beheld her, esteem and love for chastity. The grace of sanctification, says St. Thomas (3 *Dist. p.* 3, *art,* 1, *ad* 2), not only suppressed illicit concupiscence in the Virgin, but also exerted its efficacy in others ; so that although she was exceedingly graceful and beautiful no one could regard her with unlawful feeling. As in the desert those who had been bitten by serpents were restored to health by looking upon the brazen serpent erected by Moses, so those who were suffering from the stings of carnal love were refreshed and tranquillized by lifting their eyes to the purity of Mary's countenance : sinful love fled in affright before her presence.

Mary was a virgin in the three principal epochs of her life,—before she became a mother, when she became a mother, and after she became a mother. That she was a virgin before she became a mother is apparent from her words to the angel —How shall this be done, because I know not man? This objection, the Fathers teach, alluded to the vow of perpetual virginity which she had made at her presentation in the temple of Jerusalem. The objection would lose all its force had she not been already under obligation never to know man. Up to that time no maidens had been found to bind themselves to the preservation of virginity; either because they had not sufficiently considered its worth and beauty, or rather because they believed that virginity could not be severed from sterility and could not consequently be observed without reproach among the women of Israel. But the most holy Virgin,whether from humility, deeming herself unworthy to be the mother of the Savior, or from some other motive, was the first to consecrate to God by vow this virtue so acceptable in his sight, and thus devote herself body and soul, in sacrifice to him who is the sovereign giver of all good and perfect gifts. Mary, to use the phrase of the prophet (*Zach.* ix. 17), caused virgins to spring forth in two ways ; because she inspired purity into all who beheld her, and because an immense multitude of both sexes, led on by her example, vowed or observed the angelic virtue of chastity. These are the reasons why the Church in her liturgy celebrates the mother of God as mother most pure, Queen of Virgins. But the most singular feature in the virginity of Mary is that she conceived and brought forth the Savior of the world without detriment to her virginal purity. The words of the angel to Mary convince us of this greatest of all miracles. The Holy Ghost shall come upon thee, and the power of the Most High shall overshadow thee. And therefore also the Holy which shall be born of thee shall be called the Son of God; and no word shall be impossible with God (*Luke* 1). St. Chrysologus affirms, that when Mary conceived, and when she gave birth to her Son, her purity increased, her chastity was augmented, her integrity was strengthened, and her virginity confirmed (*Serm.* 122). Hence the Church salutes Mary as Mother most chaste, Mother inviolate. Mary was a virgin after she became a mother, because throughout her life she preserved that fairest of virtues which she had dedicated to God in the dawn of her days. It is true that she was espoused to Joseph, but their wedlock was altogether spiritual, celestial, and holy. In the doc-

trine of the Fathers of the Church, Joseph
was a virgin as well as Mary.   If the Savior on the cross would not recommend
his virgin mother to any but the then virgin Apostle, how could he have suffered
that her spouse should be other than a
virgin (*St. Thom. in C. I. Ep. ad Gal.*)?   It
was the wisdom of the will of God that
she who had been chosen to be the mother of the Redeemer, should be espoused
to the most just, the most pure, the most
holy man on earth.   We learn from the
Gospel that the chaste Joseph wished to
put away his spouse secretly, but was encouraged by the angel to retain her, because she had conceived by the Holy
Ghost (*Matt.* i. 20).   Then Mother forever undefiled is the Holy Virgin Mary.

II.

All that has been said of the virginity
of Mary is clearly signified in the books
of the old law.   The bush seen by Moses
in the Arabian desert which burned without being consumed, the Church assures
us was a figure of the Blessed Virgin
Mary, whose virginity always retained its
original integrity.   The fleece of Gideon,
as St. Bernard teaches (*Hom.* 2. *sup. Mis-
sus est*), was a symbol of the perfect in-

tegrity of Mary, although she gave flesh to the Divine Word. When Elias was in prayer on Mount Carmel, his servant saw a little cloud arise out of the sea like a man's foot (3 *Kings* xviii. 44). This little cloud prefigured the virgin mother of God, who arose indeed from the sea of this world, but ascended far above the world in her exemption from all the carnal infirmities of human nature. Isaias, filled with the spirit of God, caught a glimpse of Mary, and exclaimed : Behold a virgin shall conceive and bear a son, and his name shall be called Emmanuel (vii. 14). This prophecy was renewed by him under another symbol, when he said : There shall come forth a rod out of the root of Jesse, and a flower shall rise up out of his root. And the Spirit of the Lord shall rest upon him (xi. 1). This rod is the Virgin Mary, and this flower is Christ. What indicates the rod of Aaron, which budded and bloomed blossoms, and bore fruit (*Numb.* xvii. 8), unless the Blessed Virgin Mary, who conceived and brought forth her son without prejudice to her virginity ? And the eyes of the innocent dove, the flowers of the valleys, the lily among thorns, the rose of Jericho, the enclosed garden, the fountain sealed up,—what are they but symbols of the ever inviolate purity and chastity of the glorious Virgin Mary?

Why appeal on this subject to Fathers and Councils of the Church? They speak with one voice. The Apostles' Creed and the Nicene declare that the Divine Lord was conceived by the Holy Ghost of the Virgin Mary. The Councils of Lateran and Chalcedon define the same, and pronounce anathema against any one who should dare to call in question the singular chastity of Mary. When Christ was born, says St. Gregory of Nyssa (*Orat. de Nat. Christi*), he was laid in the manger; and the mother, who remained an unblemished virgin, embraced her son. Christ was born of a mother, says St. Augustine (*de Cat. Rud. c.* 22), who conceived although she knew not man, and who continued always inviolate. A virgin, she conceived; a virgin, she gave birth to her Son; a virgin, she died. Mary, we may conclude, prized most highly and preserved most singularly, beyond all other women, the virtue of chastity. She is, therefore, to be honored as the Mother of Chastity.

ASPIRATION.

Obtain for me purity of mind and body, spotless Virgin Mary.

PRACTICE.

Entreat Mary every day to number you amongst her faithful servants.

LITANY.

Read A Crown for Our Queen, by Rev. Abram J. Ryan.

SIXTEENTH DAY.

HOLINESS OF MARY.

"The king commanded that they should bring great stones, costly stones, for the foundation of the temple." 3 *Kings* v. 17.

SOLOMON, in compliance with his own promises and those of his father, undertook to build a temple to the living God; the temple when completed was a prodigy of magnificence and art. The highest power of architecture was displayed in the construction of the work, and all its parts were conspicuous for elegance of design and skill of execution. The materials were of the richest kind. Precious woods and silver and gold, elaborately wrought and disposed with consummate

taste, were scattered in profusion from
floor to roof. In the Holy of Holies were
the ark of the covenant, the altar of incense, the altar of the herds of propitiation,
the sacred vessels, and ever-lighted can-
dlesticks. Here magnificence seemed to
eclipse itself. Everything was of polished
gold. The most precious stones inter-
mingled their lustre. Whatever ingen-
uity could devise or wealth supply, was
employed to decorate the especial dwelling-place of the Most High and inspire a
sense of the splendor of his majesty. But
why speak of the glory of the famous
temple at Jerusalem? What has it to do
with Mary? In the opinion of the Fathers that temple was one of the symbols
of the sanctity of the most holy Virgin.
If the temple erected by Solomon was so
richly adorned, was it not befitting that
the living temple of the Son of God, in
which he abode for nine months in his
human nature, should be ornamented with
the sublimest brilliancy of virtue and
grace ? Let us consider now the exalted
holiness of Mary, who by a most singular
privilege was exempt from all sin, original as well as actual.

I.

It is certain that Mary is Queen of

Saints, surpassing them all in abundance of gifts, graces, and privileges granted to her by Almighty God. But the most eminent of all the gifts, graces, and privileges imparted to her is her immunity in her conception from the stain of original sin. God in his omnipotence possessed the power to enfranchise Mary from the law which involved all men in the sin of Adam, and it was exceedingly becoming that he should exercise this power in behalf of Mary. We cannot conceive the existence of a God without the attribute of infinite power. Our Savior teaches us (*Matt.* xix. 26) that with God all things are possible. The angel said to the Blessed Virgin: No word will be impossible with God (*Luke* i. 37). Job had already said (xiv. 4.): Who can make him clean that is conceived of unclean seed? Is it not thou who only art? No one can deny that God had the power and the liberty to preserve Mary from original sin. If he had, it was becoming that he should employ them. His infinite wisdom demanded that, in the incarnation of the Word, he should operate in conformity with his holiness.

What reason could there have been for denying to Mary a privilege so glorious? Should she, who was destined to be the mother of God, to receive into her bosom the most pure lily of the valleys, the Savior of the world, have been debased by the contamination of sin? Should she, who has been selected from eternity as mother of God and sanctuary of the Holy Spirit, have been subjected for a period however brief to the dominion of the Prince of Darkness? An object of divine abhorrence could she ever have been, who was full of grace, and alone amongst all women elevated to the sublimest of dignities? Was it becoming that Christ, the new Adam, should spring from a soil polluted with the malediction of sin? Can the thought be entertained for a moment that Mary was born devoid of a privilege which adorned in their origin not only the rebel angels but our first parents also, who were constituted by Almighty God in a state of rectitude and innocence? Can it be supposed that Mary was not more highly favored than Jeremias and the Baptist? They, however, were sanctified in the bosoms of their mothers.

Did Eve enjoy a more singular privilege than the mother of God? Yet Eve was formed free from the rebellion of concupiscence. Had Mary in her conception been sullied by original sin, her soul would have been disfigured, displeasing to God, unworthy of fellowship with himself and the angels, and deserving to be excluded forever from heaven. If, in that first instant, death had overtaken her she would have been lost forever, condemned forever to darkness—she who was destined to bring light to the world. She might have been compared to a star which is eclipsed at its rising, to a young rose that withers in blowing, to a fountain of grace which was choked in its origin. She would be the mother of life after having been the victim of death. Such things could not be. Almighty God, for motives less powerful than the exemption from sin of his mother, changed the course of nature, operated frequent miracles, and bestowed extraordinary favors. Did he not stop the sun in the midst of his course at the voice of Josue? Did he not recall the dead to life out of regard to Eliseus? Did he not deprive the lions of their ferocity for the protection of his servant Daniel? Did he not, contrary to the usual order of Providence, sanctify Jeremias before his birth? It is certain that the flesh of Christ is flesh of the virgin. Had she been stained with original sin it would follow that the Word, after his resurrection, glorified a flesh which in its origin was hateful to God and under the slavery of Satan. It was, finally, but just and reasonable that the Queen of Angels, who by divine promise was to crush the head of the serpent,should not be for a moment the slave of that enemy of man; otherwise he would still be able to reproach her and say to her in mockery, Behold the woman who crushed my head; but once her head was under my foot by means of originalsin, She was my slave. Behold the woman who is called all-fair and the daughter of the King of glory; but once she was deformed by sin, and I was her first king and master. Behold her who is styled the abode and mother of virtues; but first her soul was defiled by evil; I abode in her, I held dominion over her, and she was under my obedience. The force of these reasons must dissipate every doubt of the immaculate conception of the great mother of God.

But Christ came to redeem Mary as well as the other descendants of Adam, and there is no redemption where there is no original sin. Mary was indeed redeemed by Christ; but in a peculiar and more perfect manner, as was becoming in the case of her who was to give birth to the Holy of Holies and co-operate in the redemption of man. In virtue of the passion and merits of Christ, Mary was preserved by especial favor from contracting the stain of sin, whilst others are only purified from guilt already incurred. It is a greater kindness to prevent the unwary traveler from falling down a precipice than to lift him up and dress and heal his wounds after he has fallen. Did not the Savior owe this greater kindness to the mother of his predilection? Had he suffered her to be sullied by original sin, might not the impious boast that he could not, or would not, exempt her from the general law involving the children of Adam in sin? But would not this be blasphemy against the Omnipotent God? Would it not be deriding him for not making a distinction between his mother and the rest of the human family? Did not the honor of the Son of God demand that he should be born of a mother unacquainted with the servitude of sin? Was it becoming that he should descend from the all-pure bosom of his Father into a bosom once polluted with iniquity? Reason cannot tolerate the thought that Mary was conceived in sin.

One of the saddest effects of original sin is concupiscence. But the Holy Virgin, by the mercy of God, was preserved from the sting of concupiscence. We may, therefore, fairly conclude that by the same mercy she was preserved from original sin. She never experienced the tumult of the passions and the multiplicity of desires which blind us by their fury, and carry us away by their resistless impulse. She never felt the law of the members always opposing the law of the mind. She knew not the fierce war of the flesh in rebellion against the spirit. She never learned the sad lesson which experience teaches us, that it is a weary life to be in constant struggle with one's self; that there is no easy victory where man is alternately conqueror and conquered; that it is a costly triumph, where man at one time sits crowned in the triumphal car, and at another time, a captive, is led in chains before it.

If we turn to the books of the Holy Scriptures, we find Mary symbolically portrayed in the most beautiful colors as all-fair and all-pure in her conception. I will put enmities between thee and the woman, and thy seed and her seed ; she shall crush thy head (*Gen.* iii. 15). If Mary was subject to original sin, where is the perpetual enmity between her and the serpent ? Instead of crushing the head of the serpent, she herself would have been infected by his poisonous fangs. The slavery of original sin is the head of the devil. Mary crushed his head because no slavery of sin ever gained entrance into her soul (*St. Aug. in Gen.*). And does not the Church apply to the Holy Virgin the words of the Holy Spirit: Thou art all-fair, O my love, and there is no spot in thee? Open to me, my sister, my love, my dove, my undefiled (*Cant.* iv. 7 ; v. 2). Can this language be reconciled with the supposition of original sin in Mary?

We read in the Council of Trent (*Sess.* v. *ch.* 6): This Holy Synod declares that it is not its intention to comprehend in this decree, which treats of original sin, the blessed and immaculate Virgin.Mary, mother of God. If she is not included is she not excluded ? Can any other interpretation be properly attached to the words ?

It would be an endless task to undertake to quote the Fathers of the Church, who in every age expressly taught, or evidently supposed, or clearly insinuated the immunity of Mary from every blemish of sin in the first instant of her conception. Most celebrated divines, academies, and universities, continued to defend the same doctrine and disseminated their reasons through the world. Devout writers and eloquent orators proclaimed it to all the children of the Church and inculcated its acceptance. The children of Mary received the glad tidings with joy; and with gratitude to God, and pious exultation, cherished in their inmost soul the abiding belief that their dear mother, the refuge of sinners, the mother of their Savior, never remained, for one single instant, under the blighting ban of sin.

When the proper time arrived, the Holy Spirit inspired the vicar of Christ on earth to yield to the solicitation of the whole Christian world, and solemnly define, by the infallible authority with which he is invested, that the glorious Virgin Mary, mother of God, was forever unstained by sin—was immaculate in her conception. Now, therefore, we hold it as a part of our Catholic Faith that sin never dared to lift its gloating eyes to the heavenly countenance of Mary ; that when she first drew the breath of life, she drew it as the beloved one of the Father, the Son, and the Holy Ghost.

II.

The grace received by Mary, in her conception, was an exhaustless source of merit, and sanctified all the actions of her life. Divines teach that the mother of God never produced one act which did not derive its worth from that primeval grace. The seed buried in the ground germinates, grows, rises above the earth, puts forth branches, is clothed with leaves, bears blossoms, and produces fruit; but it is to the virtue of the seed that the tree owes all its glory.   In like manner the first grace received by Mary the very instant of her most pure conception, diffused its virtue through her heart and soul and her whole person, and regulated all her affections and actions. That first grace of sanctification may be regarded as the root of all the sublime favors possessed by Mary and of all the merit which she acquired. If the root be holy, so are the branches (*Rom.* xi. 16). These branches were the virtues of Mary; her good works, her worship of God, her offices of charity towards the neighbors, her practice of humility, by the constant exercise of which she was preserved from every slightest fault.

This is no mere private opinion of pious persons, of theologians, of academies, or universities, but it is a truth which cannot be called in question. The sixth Ecumenical Council, held in Constantinople, defined, and its definition was confirmed, that Mary was free from all imperfection and stain in body, soul, and understanding. The Council of Trent defined (*Sess.* vi. *can.* 23), that man could not, during his whole life, avoid all sins, also venial sins, unless by especial privilege, as the Church holds concerning the Blessed Virgin. This was always the doctrine of the Fathers of the Church. When treating of sins, says St. Augustine (*de nat. et grat. c.* 36), there is no question about the holy Virgin Mary. We know that upon her who merited to conceive and give birth to Him who could never sin, more abundant grace was bestowed that she might utterly triumph over sin. We must confess, therefore, and defend with the Angelic Doctor (1 *Sent. dis.* 44), that the Virgin Mary committed no actual sin, not even a venial sin.

ASPIRATION.

From the anger of God deliver us, Holy Virgin Mary.

PRACTICE.

Entreat the Blessed Virgin to obtain for

you sincere sorrow for all past sins, a firm resolution to avoid sin hereafter, and grace to observe it.

LITANY.

Read the "Immaculate Conception," by J. W. Bryant.

SEVENTEENTH DAY.

SORROWS OF MARY.

"Respha, the daughter of Aia, took haircloth and spread it under her upon the rock, from the beginning of the harvest till water dropped upon them, (*the children's bodies*) out of heaven: and suffered neither the birds to tear them by day, nor the beasts by night." 2 *Kings* xxi. 10.

IN the books of the old law, there is not a more admirable example of motherly love than that of Respha, mother of Armon and Miphiboseth, who were crucified by the Gabaonites out of hatred against their father Saul. After having suffered the extreme affliction of witnessing the barbarous execution of her beloved sons, she spread haircloth upon the rock and sat upon it to watch their bodies, in order to prevent the birds from tearing them by day, or the beasts by night. And it was her determination to remain there as long as life should endure. This is a symbol of the sorrow of Mary, the most tender of all mothers, who suffered the severest anguish during the life and at the death of her only Son Jesus. To Mary may be applied the lamentations of Jeremias, when he deplored the misfortunes of the holy city. To what shall I compare thee, or to what shall I liken thee, O daughter of Jerusalem? To what shall I equal thee, that I may comfort thee, O virgin daughter of Sion? For great as the sea is thy destruction. Who shall heal thee (*Lam.* ii. 13)? Mary, standing at the foot of the cross, could well have said to the passers by, O all ye that pass by the way, attend and see if there be any sorrow like to my sorrow (i. 12). Who will give water to my head, and a fountain of tears to my eyes? And I will weep day and night(*Jer.* ix. i). Call me not Noemi (that is, beautiful), but call me Mara (that is, bitter); for the Almighty hath quite filled me with bitterness (*Ruth* i. 20). In order to excite our gratitude to Mary, who offered her own heart, in union with that of her Son, as a holocaust to God for our salvation, let us endeavor to unfold the qualities of her afflictions, so that we may arrive at a knowledge of the greatness of her sorrows from the love which she bore her Son and us, and from the fortitude of soul with which she had to suffer them.

I.

The love of mothers is said to be far more ardent than that of fathers. God himself, wishing to express the kindness of his affection, compares himself to a mother (*Is.* xlix. 16). Jeremias, demanding great sorrow from the sinner, demands it similar to that of a mother who deplores the death of her only son (vi. 29). The sorrow of a mother is frequently brought forward to signify sorrow of the greatest intensity. Christ was the only Son of Mary, and she loved him more purely, more tenderly, and more fervently than other mothers love their children. Many reasons concur to demonstrate the exceeding great love of Mary for her Son. Hers was the love of a most perfect, most just, and most wise mother for a Son who was holiness by essence. Christ was her Son by the sole operation of the Holy Ghost; she loved him, therefore, with all the love of both father and mother. Entire sympathy existed between mother and Son; this produced uniformity of will, and a love so perfect that the two hearts became one; the sword that transpierced one, also transpierced the other. The thirty-three years which Mary passed with Jesus increased her love every day. His obedience, his amiability, his wisdom, the blessings which he scattered on every side, the gratitude of all classes of persons who attended him, these and a thousand other circumstances caused her love to gain daily new depth and ardor. Who, then, can describe the bitter sorrow of Mary when she beheld her Son subjected to every species of insult and torture, and expiring in innocence on a cross of shame?

But the love of nature was united in Mary with the love of charity, and this augmented exceedingly her sorrows. Other mothers love their children; but at the same time, they are bound to cherish a stronger love—love for Almighty God. In Mary the love of God was the love of her Son; for, whilst he was her Son, he was her God; and her love for God was great beyond human understanding; it was that of the creature for the Creator; of the daughter for a most affectionate father; of the spouse for her beloved one.

We must now consider the affliction, the anguish, of this mother who loved Jesus Christ as only his mother could love him. Her sorrows commenced when Simeon, taking in his arms the infant Jesus, turned to his mother and said with prophetic voice: Thy soul a sword shall pierce (*Luke* ii. 35). From that moment the passion of Christ was always before the eyes of Mary. From that moment she beheld him covered with reproaches and a sign for contradiction. In nourishing him at her bosom, she thought of the gall and vinegar which were to be presented to him in his thirst. In putting his garments around him, she thought of the cords with which he was to be bound. She looked upon his smiling countenance, and she foresaw it defiled with spittle; she saw his head crowned with thorns; his auburn hair clotted with blood; when she viewed his little feet and hands, the nails which were to fasten them to the cross were before her eyes: his heart she saw pierced by a lance. When she bent over him in his sleep with all the fondness of such a mother, his lacerated and lifeless body, which she was one day to receive in her arms, appeared in vision before her. With what feelings of agonizing love did she not press him to her heart! This martyrdom of Mary was repeated whenever she thought of the future life of her Son.

If the thought of Christ's future sufferings was martyrdom to Mary, who could fathom the ocean of her sorrows when his passion actually took place! The wounds in the body of Christ were wounds in the heart of Mary, says St. Jerome (*de B. V.*), and St. Bonaventure (*de Planctu V.*) says: What thy Son suffered in body, thou, O Virgin, didst suffer in heart. The thorns which perforated the head of her Son, the scourges which tore his flesh from his bones, the blows of the hammer, the nails, the cries of derision, were so many arrows penetrating the heart and soul of Mary. She saw her son bound, says St. Anselm (*Dial. de Pass.*), and she could not loose him; she saw him wounded, and she could not dress his wounds ; she saw his face flowing with blood, and she could not wipe it away; she wished to embrace him and it was not permitted to her. The heart of Mary, says St. Laurence Giustiniani, was a highly polished mirror, which reflected a perfect image of the passion and death of Christ. Mary, says St. Bernard, stood speechless near the cross; she was dead, and still she was living. She was dead with her Son, living with her sorrows. Mary, says St. Bernardine, was dying every moment, yet could not die. A power greater than human commanded her soul to remain united with her body.

Almighty God would not oblige Agar to

witness the death struggles of her child Ismael. When he seemed on the point of perishing from thirst Agar withdrew; for she said, I will not see the boy die (*Gen.* xxi. 16). When Noe went into the ark, the Lord shut him in on the outside (*Gen.*vii. 16) that he might not be terrified with the destruction caused by the waters of the deluge. When God commanded Abraham to offer in sacrifice his beloved son Isaac, it was not to be done in the presence of **Sara.** Why, then, was not the Almighty as thoughtful of the feelings of Mary? The intense love which existed between Jesus and Mary demanded that their hearts should share joy and sorrow in common. This is the sentiment of the Fathers of the Church. We are, moreover, frequently instructed by St. Paul, that participation in the sufferings of Christ on earth is the characteristic of the predestined to heaven. Writing to the Galatians, he places his glory in being nailed with Christ to the cross (*Gal.* ii.19). To the Philippians, he expresses his great desire to know the fellowship of the sufferings of Christ, being made conformable to his death (iii. 10). The love of Mary for Jesus, then, far greater than the love cherished for him by every apostle and every saint, called for a far deeper participation in his passion, a more thorough fellowship of his sufferings.

II.

The sorrows of Mary were excessive: but she met them with a strength of mind and firmness of heart that must excite our highest admiration and astonishment. Mary, as far as she was able, drank, draught by draught, alone with Jesus, the bitter chalice of his passion. No sooner had she heard of his capture than she endeavored to reach his presence. She followed him to the tribunals of Annas, Caiphas, Herod, and Pilate, and heard all the expressions of scorn, mockery and derision which were uttered against him. Prevented by the rabble from approaching him, she heard the blows of the scourge which fell thick and heavy upon his delicate body. She beheld him seated, with a scarlet cloak about him, as a mock king, with a reed in his hand for a sceptre, a crown of thorns upon his head, and rivulets of blood streaming down his cheeks. Having heard his condemnation, and unable to penetrate the crowd which surrounded him, she passed through the city and reached the way which mounts up to Calvary, in order to obtain a nearer view, at least, of the Lamb led to slaughter. She sees him pass, followed by the two thieves, and the instruments of his passion around Him. His members are extended upon the cross; his hands and feet are nailed to it; it is lifted up; and Christ hangs, mangled and naked, between heaven and earth, and soon languishes in death. And what does Mary do? His mother stood by the cross of Jesus (*John* xix. 25). But did she not fill the air with groans, and shrieks, and lamentations? The holy Gospel says that she stood by the cross of Jesus, and it says no more. I read of her standing by the cross, says St. Ambrose, I do not read of her weeping. *Stantem lego, flentem non lego.* With tearless eye she accompanied her Son bearing his cross to the summit of Calvary; she beheld him crucified, she heard the insults of his executioners; the lance which pierced his heart she felt penetrating her own. What constancy of soul! When she heard her Son exclaim: My God my God, why hast thou forsaken me? what a deep wound must have been opened in the heart of Mary! Every relief is denied her Son, even a drop of water to alleviate his thirst. What a trial for the constancy of Mary's afflicted heart! Jesus yields up his spirit; and Mary says within her agonizing soul: O my Son, who

will give to me that I may die for thee!
The Son dies; why does not the sorrowful
mother die with thee (*Bern. de Planet.* v.) ?
Tears and sighs temper sorrow, but grief
which speaks not whispers the over-
fraught heart and bids it break. So it was
with Mary. When Jesus expired, all nature was thrown into agitation; the veil of
the temple was rent in two from the top
even to the bottom; and the earth quaked,
and the rocks were rent, and the graves
were opened, and the bodies of the saints
that had slept arose (*Matt.* xxvi. 51). All
nature was convulsed, but the holy Virgin stood immovable in her sorrow.

But whence the wonderful constancy
of Mary in the passion of her Son? It
was the result of conformity with the
will of God, who required full satisfaction
for our sins. Adequate satisfaction for the
sins of man could be rendered to an offended God by him only who was both
God and man. Such was Jesus, the Son
of Mary. Jesus submitted willingly to the
pleasure of his Father, and offered to him
an infinite treasure of sufferings and merit
for our redemption and salvation. Mary,
being wholly submissive to the will of
God, could not oppose the passion of her
Son. Mary, moreover, besides being the
mother of God was our mother also and

given to us as a mother by Christ on the cross.

The mother must desire the welfare of her children; our welfare required that Christ should suffer and die for our redemption; Mary, therefore, with unshaken firmness, in spite of every natural feeling, willingly accepted the passion of her Son.

ASPIRATION.

Holy Mother, impress the wounds of thy Son, my Savior, upon my heart.

PRACTICE.

Say the beads, reflecting on the dolorous mysteries of the Rosary.

LITANY.

Read Faber's Bethlehem.

EIGHTEENTH DAY.

MARY, MOTHER OF SINNERS.

"I will go into the field and glean the ears of corn that escape the hands of the reapers, wheresoever I shall find grace with a householder that will be favorable to me." *Ruth* ii. 2.

THE kind-hearted Ruth, having arrived in the neighborhood of Bethlehem from the land of Moab, and seeking to relieve the distressed circumstances of Noemi, said to her: I will go into the field and glean the ears of corn that escape the hands of the reapers, wheresoever I shall find grace with a householder that will be favorable to me. She then went to the field of Booz, a man of wealth and high condition, and, with permission, followed industriously the footsteps of the reapers and gathered the ears of corn that escaped their hands.

This is a simple historical fact recorded in the books of the old law ; but sacred expositors regard it as full also of mystic and symbolic meaning. Booz, they say, represents God; the reapers, those charged with the care of souls ; the ears of corn which escaped the reapers' hands, hardened and inveterate sinners, who elude the zeal of the ministers of God and become an easy prey to the vultures of the abyss. Ruth is a figure of Mary, the most benign mother of God, through whose powerful intercession the most incorrigible sinners are affectionately invited to pardon and happiness. As Ruth found favor in the eyes of Booz, says St. Bonaventure, so Mary found favor in the eyes of the Savior; the ears of corn, that is, the souls abandoned by the reapers,

she can allure to penance, lead to pardon,
and the possession of heaven. Mary is
the kind mother of sinners, because she
obtains for them repentance and pardon ;
and because through her intercession
sinners attain the glory of paradise.

I.

To acquire a thorough understanding
of the great benefit,which the sinner obtains from God by means of Mary, when
he rises from the state of sin to the state
of grace, we must consider attentively and
calmly what sin itself is. Mortal sin is a
transgression of the eternal law, an injury done by the creature to the sovereign
majesty of the Creator; it is a rebellion
of man against God by which man subjects himself to Satan, the most cruel of
tyrants ; it is a renouncement of eternal
happiness for the sake of eternal misery.
Whatever can be conceived most extrav-
agant, most hideous, most horrible, furnishes but a faint idea of sin. God hates
sin as much as he loves himself. The
same reasons for which he, of necessity,
loves himself, force him to detest and
abominate sin, infinitely opposed to himself. The love of God for himself is,
therefore, the reason and measure of his
hatred of sin. As God loves himself with

an eternal love, and there never was a
moment in which he did not love himself,
so he detests sin with eternal detestation,
and there never was a moment in which
he did not detest it.   God loves himself
by necessity of his nature; he necessarily therefore abominates sin, and can no
more cease to abominate it than he can
cease to be God.   God loves himself with
infinite love; he could not love himself
with love more intense; his hatred for sin
is, therefore, infinite; he could not pursue it with greater hatred.   The sacred
writings are filled with examples of the
hatred of God against sin.   Lucifer,
the noblest of the angels, rebelled in his
pride against God, and drew into his rebellion a third part of the angelic host;
God stretched forth his right hand in anger, and precipitated them all into the
abyss of hell.   Adam and Eve sinned a-
gainst God by disobedience, and God without delay despoiled them of original justice, banished them from the paradise of
pleasure, let loose in their hearts the rest-
lessness of concupiscence and fury of
their passions, to deprive them even in
this life of all tranquillity of soul.   God
punished with eternal death Cain, the
murderer of his brother.   For their iniquities the Lord overwhelmed all the gen-

erations of men with the waters of the
deluge, and rained down brimstone and
fire from heaven upon Sodom and Gomorrha. Countless other examples are
recorded in Scripture of the chastisements
for sin inflicted upon men by Almighty
God. The prophets portray in the most
vivid colors the injury which is done to
God by sin and the indignation of the
Almighty against the sinner. And
whence all the evils which inundate the
earth—crimes tempest, earthquakes, the
thirst of wild beasts for human blood, war,
famine, pestilence, diseases, death—
whence hell itself for man, if not from the
sins of man, from man's disobedience to
his God ?

The greatest punishment with which
God can visit sinful man on earth is the
withdrawal of grace and light from on
high ; for want of which man goes wandering and stumbling in the dark, unable
to discern the way which leads to heaven.
And this is a punishment which is soon
felt by the sinner. But is there no resource for him ? There is, and it is Mary.
She incessantly repeats to the sinner: I
am the mother of fair love, and of fear,
and of knowledge, and of holy hope. In
me is all grace of the way, and of the
truth ; in me is all hope of life, and of vir-

tue (*Eccl.* xxiv. 24). Mary is our mother and loving mother, and was bequeathed to us as a mother by Jesus, her Son, expiring on the cross for our redemption. The especial care and solicitude of Mary, our mother, for her children, has reference to their eternal salvation. It is the duty of a mother to watch over, nourish, and instruct her children. If she sees her son in danger of falling down a precipice, she flies on the wings of love to withdraw him from danger; if he is taken ill and she sees him in danger of death, she knows no rest, day nor night, until his health is re-established. Mary guards Christians by her patronage, she nourishes them with holy thoughts, and instructs them by the light of grace in their duties to Almighty God. If one of her children, from perverse inclination or transport of passion or violence of temptation, falls into sin, or, what is far worse, by repeated acts becomes habituated to sin and lies in sluggish and stupid repose in the arms of iniquity, Mary, full of anxiety, presents herself before the throne of her Son, and ceases not to ask, to beg, and to pray, until the slumberer is aroused, until the grace of repentance has been vouchsafed to her unfortunate child. Mary, by giving birth to Jesus, introduced life into the world and is justly called the mother of the living (*S. Ephr. de Laud. Deip.*); and as Jesus is the life, Mary is the mother of life.

Mary is the mother of life even for those who, lying immersed in iniquities, know not what to do or whither to turn. These miserable sinners may be compared to mariners, who, being overtaken by a tempest in the midst of the ocean and tossed to and fro by the fury of the winds during the darkness of the storm, lose their course and know not in what direction to steer. Unexpectedly the clouds divide, the polar star appears, their courage revives, the course is pointed out to them, and they are saved from shipwreck. The Fathers of the Church teach that Mary is the beneficent star that sheds light over the path of heaven for the sinner; and the Church hence salutes her, Hail, Star of the Sea. It is not the merits of the sinner, for merits he has none, but the tender love of our amiable mother, which obtains for him light and grace to be converted and live a life of virtue on earth, and thus merit a life of happiness in heaven.

God is indignant against the sinner, and if he is slow to vengeance, he is slow out of mercy, that he may see whether

the sinner will at last listen to the reproaches with which conscience still continues to load him. Mary, aware of the
blindness and the danger of the sinner and
of the eternal pains already prepared for
his crimes, with feelings of motherly compassion says to her Son Jesus: They have
no wine. Only Son of my bosom, that
sinner my son too by adoption, given to
me by thyself, is in want of the wine of
grace. Jesus, who knew not how to refuse to his mother a temporal favor on
earth, much less knows how to refuse her
in heaven a favor which regards the
eternal salvation of a soul redeemed by
his own blood. St. Peter Damian (*Serm.*
i. *de Nat.*) says, that the treasures of divine mercy are in the hands of Mary and
that she disposes them to whoso she
wishes. A striking image of what has
been said is found in that which is related
in the first book of Kings of Abigail and
David. There was in the wilderness of
Maon a man by the name of Nabal,
whose possessions were in Carmel. He
was very wealthy, possessing three thousand sheep and a thousand goats. But he
was foolish, rough and harsh in his man-
ners, and ungrateful to David who had
protected his property in the wilderness.

When the servants of David applied to

him for food in the name of their master, he dismissed them with an insulting answer. Abigail, as prudent as fair, foreseeing the coming vengeance of David, hastened to meet him in order to anticipate the effects of his indignation. Prostrate at the feet of David, she said to him : regard not, I pray, this naughty man Nabal; for according to his name, he is a fool, and folly is with him (1 *Kings* xxv. 25). David, appeased by the entreaties of Abigail, abstained from shedding blood and taking vengeance of Nabal, and said to Abigail: go in peace into thy house; behold, I have heard thy voice, and have honored thy face. In this fact, explained allegorically by the Fathers, Nabal represents the sinner, David, God, and Abigail the Virgin Mary. Mary by her fervent intercession, wards off from foolish sinners the blows of divine indignation, obtains for them a return to the life of grace, and of children of wrath, makes them children of God. Mary is therefore, the mother of sinners, because she interests herself assiduously in their behalf, obtains for them sorrow for their follies and crimes, and leads them back to God and the life of grace.

II.

Man by sin becomes an enemy of God, and God in just punishment of his crime, despoils him of grace and leaves him in the hands of his wickedness and blind passions; and if he dies in his sins, he is hurled into the abyss, there to undergo eternal torments. If, through the intercession of Mary, the sinner lives again to grace, she extends to him still further patronage, in order that he may close his days in the peace of the Lord and enter upon the enjoyment of an imperishable life of glory in heaven. Here it is proper to observe that as soon as by means of divine grace we are rendered adopted children of God, we have communicated to us a right to the eternal kingdom of heaven and to all the spiritual favors which are necessary for its attainment. For, as the Apostle says (*Gal.* iv. 7.), if children we are also heirs. When God infuses grace into our souls, in order that it may be a perfect mark of our adoption he gives us a right to his kingdom, and makes us, as children, heirs of all his spiritual blessings. As the grace which is gratuitously conferred upon us to exalt us to the quality of children of God, is the principle of spiritual life within us, it also enables all our actions to become actions of life, having reference to eternal life and endowed with value for the acquisition of celestial glory. Since we acquire grace through the beneficent intercession of Mary, it follows that Mary is, to the repentant sinner, the mother of grace on earth, and the guide to glory in heaven. What a consoling thought that the most holy Virgin is our mother! Grace! Glory! Peerless treasures! Yet the one and the other we obtain through Mary. Well does the Church honor her with the noble denomination of Gate of Heaven. Even to the heart of the unfortunate sinner is it consoling, when, standing on the threshold of the church on festive occasions, he hears the ministers of God chanting joyfully in honor of Mary—O happy Gate of Heaven.

All that has been said of Mary is registered in the writings of the Fathers of the Church, Greek as well as Latin. A few only can be mentioned. St. Peter Damian (*de. B. V.*), reflecting upon the blessings and graces imparted to sinners through the mediation of Mary, with holy exultation styles her the Ladder of Heaven, because, says the Saint, by Mary God descended from heaven to earth, in order that by her men might mount from earth to heaven. St. Thomas (*Opusc.* 8), assigning the reason why the Church honors Mary under the symbol of Star of the Sea, says: As mariners are guided to port by a star, so Christians are guided to heaven by Mary. St. Bernard (*Serm. de S. M.*) says: The ark of Noe signifies the Ark of Grace; that is, the Virgin Mary; for, as by means of the ark Noe and his family escaped the deluge, so by means of Mary sinners escape the shipwreck of sin. Noe built the ark in order that he might save himself from the waters of the deluge; Christ prepared Mary for himself in order that he might redeem the human race. By means of the ark, eight persons only were preserved; by means of Mary, all are invited to salvation. Let us conclude with St. Anastasius of Antioch (*Serm. i. de Annunt.*): Hail, full of grace, for us the way of salvation and the ascent to heaven and place of repose and tabernacle of refreshment.

ASPIRATION.

Deliver us from eternal death, holy Virgin Mary.

PRACTICE.

As soon as you fall into any fault, pray

the Blessed Virgin to obtain pardon for you from God.

LITANY.

Read "Little Month of May."

NINETEENTH DAY.

THE GOODNESS OF OUR LADY.

"Who is she that cometh forth as the morning rising?"   *Cant.* vi. 9.

DURING the darkness of the night, business, commerce, all the stirring affairs of life, are in repose. But when night approaches its close, the young shepherd rises from his couch of straw, puts on his humble garments, and ascends the mountain side. When he reaches the summit, he turns his eyes to the east, and at the first glimmer of the morning light he strikes up a joyful strain to welcome the rosy dawn. Dreary is the night, and particularly during the gloom of winter; but most dreary was the night of the Old Testament, prolonged for forty centuries. After our first parents had extinguished by sin the vivifying light of grace, darkness, in the words of the prophet,covered the earth (*Is.* lx. 2). The patriarchs, the prophets, and the souls of the departed just, were sighing in the expectation of rising day, and gave vent to their sorrow by frequently exclaiming: O Sun of Justice, when wilt thou rise above us, thou beneficent bearer of light, to illuminate our souls lying here in prison and darkness! For a long time, heaven was inexorable. But now the oracles of the prophets were heard no more; the sceptre of Juda had passed to the hands of a stranger; the years of the prophecy of Daniel were approaching their termination; and the redemption of the human race appeared to be imminent. Suddenly, like the lightning flash breaking through the obscurity of night, a light, as of morning, was seen,and the festive chant of angels was heard, who sang their applause and interrogated one another: Who is she that cometh forth as the morning rising? Who is she, who by the effulgence of her splendor eclipses all the stars of the firmament? Who is she who, becoming the benefactress of mortals, bears alleviation to the sick and weak? Who is she, who with fresh-falling dew moistens the earth and renders it fruitful? Who is she, who putting wild beasts and robbers to flight, makes secure the way of the traveler? Why, O blessed angels, are you astonished? What is the cause of your wonder? Do you not believe that God established, as the principle of salvation for all men past and future, belief in Jesus Christ incarnate, and that the same God foretold to Adam and Eve that a woman would crush the head of the serpent? Are you unacquainted with the prophetic declaration that a virgin would conceive and bring forth the Messias? Mary, the most holy Mother of God, is that light, which, gleaming before your eyes like a sparkling aurora on the day of her nativity, shortly after came to us the bearer of the divine source of splendor, the only-begotten Son of God. Exult, O lovers of the Virgin, and let your hearts be inundated with the purest joy to the universal world. Let us, adhering to the symbol of the dawn, explain the motives of exultation, the prerogatives and privileges of Mary.

I.

The first property of the dawn is, that it·surpasses in brilliancy all the stars of the firmament. It is indeed delightful to the view and pleasant to the soul to turn the eyes to the heavens in a still and cloudless night. It is a spectacle worthy of admiration, to observe so many constellations arrayed in regular bands; so many heavenly bodies, different in size, and distinguished by varying degrees of splendor, regularly accomplishing their allotted course. A night of such brightness scarce yields in lustre to day itself. But at the first blush of morning the light of the gleaming stars begins to grow pale; by degrees it is extinguished and a veil seems to be drawn over all the beauties of the night. Those stars are the angels and the immense bands of saints. But they all, though effulgent with holiness, disappear in the presence of Mary. The angels are pure spirits, and their splendor is so overpowering that mortal eye could not sustain it. An angel wrestled with Jacob during the whole night, but at the approach of morning he requested to be released. Let me go, for it is break of day (*Gen.* xxxii. 26). But why ask to be let go because it was break of day? Was not he an angel of light? As the stars hide themselves at the coming of the light of the sun, the angel was abashed by the presence of Mary, of whom the morning rising was a figure. Mary is so resplendent with supernatural light, says St. Peter

Damian (*Serm.* 20), that, like the dawn, she excels the brightness of all other celestial beings, and they are as if they were not when she appears.

The Patriarchs were great and glorious by virtue and faith, but in virtue and faith they were far surpassed by Mary. The Prophets were distinguished for their power of foretelling future events, but Mary is their Queen. The apostles, the confessors, the anchorites, acquired great glory by watchings, fastings, labors, austerities, and other good works; but their glory cannot compare with the glory of Mary. Sublime is the glory of the martyrs, with their palms in their hands and their crowns on their heads; but Mary is the greatest of all martyrs, and of them all she is the Queen. Agatha, Cecilia, Agnes, Theresa, and the innumerable array of holy virgins, seem incomparably fair and beyond competition in merit; but when we turn our eyes to Mary, the Queen of Virgins, never sullied by the slightest stain of sin, we exclaim: Who is she that cometh forth as the morning rising? What does she say of herself? From the beginning, and before the world, was I created; and unto the world to come I shall not cease to be; and in the holy dwelling-place I have ministered before him. I took root in an honorable people,and in the portion of my God his inheritance; and my abode is in the full assembly of Saints (*Eccl.* xxiv. 14). What wonder, then, says St. Peter Damian (*Serm.* 3, *in Nat. V.*), if the praises of the holy Virgin defy the power of the human language, since she transcends in sublimity of merit human nature itself ? Patriarchs and prophets, apostles and martyrs, with all their triumphs around them,cannot equal the grandeur of Mary, for she possessed the virtues of them all united; she was enriched with the plenitude of the treasures of divine grace.

Another property of the dawn is to bring relief to the sick; for to them the morning is as cheering as the night is wearisome. As far as regards infirmities of the body, sacred shrines in every part of the Christian world bear witness, by thousands of votive tablets, to the boundless kindness of Mary. There are to be seen the grateful acknowledgment of persons afflicted with every species of human ailment; through the mediation of Mary they recovered health and vigor of body and buoyancy of spirit.

But let us rather speak of spiritual infirmities, of sins which lacerate the soul and subject it to the slavery of Satan. Sin, being opposed to the supernatural light and efficacy of grace, involves man in darkness, and breaking the force of the mind, renders it languid and infirm, so that it is unable to distinguish what is truly good, and love it and pursue it. But O the kindness of Mary towards poor, unfortunate sinners! What one of them had ever humble recourse to her and met with a repulse? Mary by her intercession infuses light into the darkness of the sinner who is walking in the shadow of death, in order that he may be enabled to discover his faults and iniquities. The mercy of Mary, says St. Bonaventure (*in Spec. c.* 8), was great when she was an exile on earth, but it is far greater now, when she is reigning triumphant in heaven. She displays it now more fully, because from her throne on high she discerns far greater necessities. From the light of her mercy on earth, she may be called fair as the moon; but from the splendor of the mercy which she now exhibits, she is to be called bright as the sun. Upon whom does not the sun shine? It shines impartially upon the just and the unjust. So Mary is ready to give ear to the prayers of all men, and presses to her bosom with motherly feeling the repentant sinner. She is that Sun of Mercy that causes the rays of divine grace to reach all the children of Adam (*St. Bernard. de Verb. Apoc.*). Who, now, will not think of Mary? Who will not love her who kindly obtains for us pardon and grace? She is a lamp to our feet in the doubtful paths of life; she is relief to our heart in its anxieties, our solace in affliction, our refuge in temptation and danger; after her only Son, and with virtue derived from him, she is salvation to the faithful. But whilst sinners have every motive to confide in the holy Virgin, this is not to be understood of those sinners who, with obstinate impiety, bend their neck voluntarily under the yoke of their iniquities, because they imagine that Mary will be always their protectress. Mary is not the protectress and advocate of the willing slaves of wickedness, but of repentant sinners who wish to return to the bosom of their Father and God.

Another property of dawn is to render the earth fruitful by refreshing dews intrusted to its dispensing hands. Mary has the dispensing of the treasures of heaven; and upon men, through her, descend celestial favors. Mary is a treasury, says Richard of St. Lawrence, because in her the Almighty has deposited all the gifts of his grace; and from this treasury he draws bountiful pay for his valiant soldiers.   Do you know to which side Jesus, when expiring, inclined his head?   To the side, says Cardinal Hugo, on which his mother stood.   And why? To point out to us to whom we should have recourse in our necessities after his death; that is, to Mary.

The Lord commanded Moses to add to the ark of the testimony the propitiatory, which was to be made of the purest gold; thence God promised to give orders and speak to him (*Ex.* xxv. 17–22).   This propitiatory, according to a sacred commentator, was a figure of Mary.   From her the Lord speaks to the hearts of men, grants pardon, imparts graces; from her all good flows to man.   Mary became the treasurer of divine grace by containing within herself the Author of grace, and she is also the dispenser of heavenly favors.   Hence we may conclude with St. Bernard (*in Sign. Mag.*), that from the fulness of Mary all receive; the slave, ransom; the diseased, health; the afflicted, consolation; the sinner, pardon; the just man, grace; the angel, joy; and the Most Holy Trinity, glory.

II.

The fourth property of dawn is, that it dissipates by its brightness the darkness of night; lays open dangers hidden before, and puts to flight thieves and robbers. Thieves and robbers station themselves in the night by the wayside, and lie in wait for the traveler in order to strip him of his property; the demon spreads his nets and weaves his plans in order to despoil man of the grace of God. Although Lucifer experienced a ruinous defeat when he was driven from heaven forever and precipitated into the abyss of hell, he still retains that envious malignity which he had in the beginning; and not being able to satisfy it by rising up against God himself, he wages war with all his power against the favored creatures of God. He never indulges repose, but is always busied in sending forth his emissaries against the whole human family; so that we, already wounded in the soul by original sin, find ourselves under the necessity of joining battle with these hellish foes, and the fight has no end till life is extinct. We are all subject to temptation; even the great apostle saw another law in his members fighting against the law of his mind, and captivating him in the law of sin (*Rom.* vii. 23): he had given to him an angel of Satan, to buffet him (2 *Cor.* xii. 7).St. Peter(*I. Ep.* v. 8) exhorted the faithful to be sober and watch; because their adversary, the devil, as a roaring lion, was going about, seeking whom he might devour. But how escape his wiles and avoid surprise, since he lies concealed like a serpent and watches the favorable moment to strike, and even transforms himself sometimes into an angel of light? He would indeed lead thousands of souls every day into the depths of perdition, but thanks to Mary, the mystic aurora, the darkness spread around by the wicked spirits is dissipated, and we are enabled to elude their wiles and triumph over sin. The spirits of darkness, grown powerful through Eve, are scattered in flight through Mary (*S. Bern.*). From Eve we have death and darkness, from Mary, life and light. Eve was conquered by the treacherous demon; Mary conquered and bound him, and like a slave he is forced to obey this most powerful queen (*S. Ber. in Sig. Mag.*). The palm is the symbol of victory; and Mary is seated upon a throne in heaven, conspicuous to all engaged in combat, like a lofty palm, signifying the victory which all may gain who array themselves under her protection. I was exalted like a palm tree in Cades (*Eccl.* xxiv. 18). Holofernes, a symbol of Satan, with his Assyrian soldiers, was besieging the city of Bethulia. Mary

behaves in a similar manner with regard to
Christians when they are assailed by temptation. Let us therefore conclude with St.
Bonaventure (*in Spec.*), in the same manner that thieves and robbers take to flight
at the first break of dawn, as if the image
of death appeared before them, so the
infernal enemies turn and flee when they
discover that their schemes are laid open
by the kindness and mercy of Mary.

ASPIRATION.

Mother, in thy kindness, pray for us all.

PRACTICE.

Make an act of sincere contrition for
all your sins.

LITANY.

Read " The Foot of Cross" by Fr. Faber.

———

TWENTIETH DAY.

MARY, MOTHER OF HUMILITY.

"While the king was at his repose, my spikenard sent forth the odor thereof." *Cant.* i. 11.

IN reading the inspired books of Scripture, our hearts are so fired with divine
love, and our minds so filled with spirit-

ual sweetness, that we seem to have a-
bandoned earth, and to find ourselves
rapt in ecstasy in the blessed region of
the contemplatives in heaven. The Gospels are all sublime; but the Gospel of St.
John is conspicuous with a glory peculiar
to itself. This holy apostle, in his first
flight, rose to the bosom of Almighty God,
and there contemplated the Eternal Word,
the majesty of the only-begotten, by
whom all things were made, and without
whom was made nothing that was made.
If amongst the Gospels the most sublime
is that of St. John, the book of Canticles
is the most sublime of all the books of
the Old Testament. Its very title, Canticle of Canticles, points to its meaning hidden in the words, and manifests its transcendent sublimity; for whilst in this nup-
tial Canticle the tender love and affectionate expressions of two spouses are
reported, the Fathers and sacred expositors assure us that God, the Church, the
just soul, and especially the Blessed Virgin are mystically signified. Mary is undoubtedly prefigured in the spouse, because she is among the other saints as the
moon among the stars; because the incarnation of the Word, and consequently
his espousals with the Church, were
accomplished in her and by her means;

and because the flesh of Christ, assumed by the Word, was the flesh of the Virgin Mary,—hence, when the Word united flesh with himself, he, in a manner, united with himself the most holy Virgin (*Corn. a Lap.*). In the book of Canticles every phrase, every expression, every word, coming from God and tending to God, inspires holiness, respect, and veneration. If you ask of the Fathers of the Church what the meaning is of those words of the spouse of the Canticles, While the king was at his repose, my spikenard sent forth the odor thereof, they will reply, that by the spikenard is signified the humility of Mary, which pleased God so much that he took flesh in her bosom. We have already touched upon the subject of which we intend to treat in the present consideration —the profound humility of Mary of which the spikenard was a symbol. As the spikenard is a rare perfume, the delicious fragrance of which attracts the admiration of the passers by, so the humility of Mary, raising its sweetness even to heaven, moved the Almighty, turned towards her his gaze, and induced him to select her for his mother (*St. Bon. in Spec. ch.* 4). That we may learn from Mary to cultivate this heavenly virtue, let us consider the fruits which it produced in her, and the manner to practise it.

I.

There are two kinds of humility—the one of mind, the other of heart. This virtue has three principal degrees. The first degree consists, not only in feeling our nothingness before God, and that of ourselves we possess nothing but misery and weakness, but also in disesteeming ourselves, and reputing ourselves unworthy of the esteem of men. The second consists in bearing with patience the contempt of others. The third loves reproaches and injuries and goes in search of them. This is the manner in which it is necessary to proceed in order to assimilate ourselves to the Son of God, despised and vilified.

Amongst all the virtues most constantly exercised by our divine Savior, the first is humility. From the first breath that he drew in his mother's bosom till his last sigh upon the cross, all his footsteps were marked with humility and humiliation. He chose to be born of a poor and humble mother; in his circumcision he assumed the character of a sinner; he passed thirty years almost wholly unknown in the shop of an artisan; he was afterwards regarded with disdain, and cruelly persecuted by those for whom he had given innumerable proofs of benevolence. The Holy Virgin, after Jesus Christ, loved and cultivated in the highest degree this incomparable virtue.

It is related by the holy Fathers that Mary, a child of three years of age, began to manifest her humility, when by divine inspiration she presented herself at the temple, and dedicated herself to Almighty God. She knew that she herself and all other creatures belonged entirely to God; but she wished to make a solemn attestation of her subjection, by pronouncing in his honor a vow of perpetual virginity. By this act Mary abandoned the world, withdrew from the eyes of men, and retired from her parents in order to unite herself more intimately with God. She renounced the hopes of the Hebrew women, who were all ambitious of the fortune of giving birth to the Messias, and esteemed it a disgrace to be destitute of posterity. Mary, to give herself entirely to God, sacrificed to him, also, her individual liberty, so that she might have said to the Almighty: Lord, Thou hast not wished from me holocausts or victims; the blood of bulls and goats was not pleasing to thee. Behold me, O Lord, prompt to hearken to the voice of thy holy inspiration, and to offer in sacrifice my body and soul, and subjecting myself utterly to thy most holy pleasure. This sacrifice was most acceptable to God; and Mary, as was said of the Saviour, increased in wisdom, and age, and grace with God and men (*Luke* ii. 52).

Mary was pleasing to God on account of her virginity, but on account of her humility she was chosen to be his mother, says St. Bernard (*Hom. sup.Miss. est.*). The Spouse of the Canticles says to his spouse: Thou hast wounded my heart, my sister, my spouse, thou hast wounded my heart with one hair of thy neck (*Cant.* iv. 9). This one hair of the neck of the spouse, according to Rupertus, was the humble opinion which Mary had of herself, with which she wounded the heart of God. When the time appointed for the redemption of man had arrived, the Angel Gabriel was sent to the lowly Virgin Mary to announce to her that she was to be the mother of God. She well understood the sublime dignity proffered to her but in her humility she declined it, alleging as a motive that she had consecrated her virginity to Almighty God, and could not, without guilt, violate her promise. Satisfied that her virginity would remain inviolate, she signified her acceptance of the dignity of mother of God by saying: Behold the handmaid of the Lord. O wonderful, profound humility of Mary! One of the noblest of the angels engages in conversation with her; he salutes her as full of grace, and promises her that the Holy Ghost shall come upon her. Mary is elevated to the honor of the mother of God; she is preferred to all creatures; she is made queen of heaven and earth; still, instead of being puffed up with pride, she bends her eyes and head to the earth, and humbly says: Behold the handmaid of the Lord. There is no great difficulty to be humble in abjection, but to preserve humility in the midst of honors is most exalted virtue. The greater thou art, the more humble thyself in all things, and thou shalt find grace before God, says Ecclesiasticus (ii. 20). Mary followed this advice and her glory was in proportion. The more lofty an edifice is to be, the deeper should be the foundations, and the more we are devoted to holy humility, the greater will be our glory. We on the contrary, if fortune favors us with honors, forget what we were before. We esteem ourselves great and worthy, because men who are led by external appearances alone, attach greatness and worthiness to the position which we occupy.

Mary, after having conceived by the Holy Ghost, went into the mountainous country with haste, into a city of Juda, to visit her cousin Elizabeth. This visit in Mary was not a mere matter of curiosity, but a mystery in which her humility shone forth conspicuously. She no longer calls herself the handmaid of the Lord, but exhibits herself as the servant of the creature. She humbles herself to others when she might justly elevate herself above them. She comports herself as a servant, when she has been invested with the right of commanding all creatures. Elizabeth was filled with wonder at the visit of Mary; but what is more surprising, she went not to be ministered to, but to console, congratulate, and minister to Elizabeth. The more she was enriched with heavenly favors the more Mary humbled herself, never forgetting that all she possessed was a gratuitous gift of God. St. Bernard very appropriately remarks, that, after the Son of God, no creature was ever so highly exalted as Mary, because none other ever descended to the depths of Mary's humility. It is easy now to understand that the love of humility besides obtaining the love of God and the treasures of his grace, conquers the principal and worst of vices, the source of all

evils and sins on the authority of the
Holy Ghost.   And this vice, this perennial source of sin, is pride. The humble
man also, is master of himself; for he
easily quells the tumult of passion and
thus secures that peace of heart which
immeasurably surpasses all earthly joy.

II.

But in what manner did Mary exercise
humility? As was before observed, there
are two species of humility—the one of understanding, or judgment, and the other
of will.   Humility of judgment, according
to St. Bernard, consists in thinking humbly of ourselves, and esteeming ourselves
the vile, miserable creatures which we are
in reality.   It is certain, by a truth, that
of ourselves we are a mere nothing—we
are foolish, unsuited for operating virtuously; we can claim, as our own, only defects
and sins, and this should make us consider
ourselves less than nothing. We live, we
move, and we are, because God so wishes
it, and all the good that we perform a-
rises from virtue communicated to us by
Almighty God.   Without him we can do
nothing.   The truly humble view themselves according to this truth; they appropriate to themselves nothing but evils,
they are unwilling to receive the praises
of men, they believe themselves worthy
of blame, they think that derision and con-

tempt are what they deserve; and thus they become most dear to the Almighty. The more worthless a man is in his own estimation, says St. Gregory, the more precious **he** becomes in the eyes of God. Humility of will consists in desiring to be disesteemed, and taking pleasure in injuries and insults. This humility is more meritorious because we gain more before God by the acts of the will than by those of the understanding, and this is the humility of heart which our Savior taught by word and example. Learn of me because I am meek and humble of heart (*Matt.* xi. 29).

From what has been already said, it is evident that Mary was assiduous in the practice of humility of both will and understanding. But one of the most luminous examples of humility of will is that which she left us in her purification. Mary was the fairest, the purest, the most highly privileged of all mere creatures; she was the mother of the eternal Word made man. She was conceived and born in holiness; she grew like a fruitful olive in the house of the Lord, enjoying his perpetual benediction ; she conceived by the Holy Ghost, and brought forth her Son without pain, without prejudice to her virginal purity. Still she voluntarily submitted to the law which had been imposed upon other women to present themselves at the temple for purification. From the love which she cherished for the fairest of virtues, virginity, we may readily conclude what a sacrifice she made on the day of her purification by appearing before the public as a woman sullied with sin. Mary thought not of her privileges ; it was enough for her that she was exercising an act of humility and religion. Her Son submitted to the law of circumcision, although the Lord of the law; and she wished to submit to the law of purification, although not bound by its provisions. After the example of Christ, can greater examples of humility and self-abasement be found than those which Mary has bequeathed to us ?

ASPIRATION.

Holy Mother, teach me *true* humility.

PRACTICE.

Avoid self-praise, and bear blame patiently.

LITANY.

Read "Life of Our Lady" by M. P.

TWENTY-FIRST DAY.

POWER OF MARY.

"Blessed be thy speech, and blessed be thou, who hast kept me to-day from coming to blood, and revenging me with my own hand." 1 *Kings* xxv. 33.

MARY is not only a loving mother to those who devoutly honor her, but she is also the mother of sinners; for this reason, as is indicated in the conduct of Abigail, a figure of Mary, she exerts herself continuously to soften the divine anger justly enkindled against us when we fall into sin. David, in the wilderness of Pharan, being destitute of food, asked of Nabal, a very wealthy man, the provisions necessary for the sustenance of himself and his companions. Nabal gave a churlish refusal to the servants of David, and added to the refusal reproaches and contempt. This conduct excited the anger of David, and taking with himself four hundred armed men, he set out for the house of Nabal, swearing to exterminate him and his whole family. But the prudent Abigail met David with presents, and appeased by her entreaties his indignation against Nabal. David, grown calm, exclaimed: Blessed be thy speech, and blessed be thou, who hast kept me to day from coming to blood, and revenging me with my own hand. Go in peace into thy house; behold! I have heard thy voice, and have honored thy face. Let us now reflect upon the mystical signification of this scriptural narrative. God requires of sinners the worship which is due to him, and the performance of good works, but he receives from them instead, offences and insults. Justly indignant, he determines to take signal vengeance of his impious creatures. But the blow of destruction is about to descend, when Mary, the mystic Abigail, prostrates herself at the feet of her Son, and says to him: Calm thyself, my Son, calm thyself. Thou mightest justly punish the rebellious sinner, because he denies to thee the homage of subjection and love to which thou hast a right, but even if he has disregarded his duty, I will not resign my office of advocate of sinners. If thou seest them deficient in good works, consider the abundance of merits in me, thy mother. Whilst thou wast in agony on the cross, thou freely gavest me to all sinners for a mother. I regard them as my adopted children. Can a mother forget her offspring? No, never.

Then, until they have made their peace with thee, I will continue to protect them. Mary, in this manner, intercedes for sinners, and every day many return to God. Let us consider, now, that Mary is powerful for the salvation of all, and more especially for the salvation of repentant sinners.

I.

There exists no more frightful monster than sin. It creates such disorder and deformity in the soul, that the Almighty, were he not restrained by his mercy, would immediately inflict the most fearful chastisements upon the sinner. In the beginning, the angels were created and adorned with extraordinary holiness and grace; they were resplendent like stars, and Lucifer in their midst shone like the sun. But pride took possession of a large number of them, and they rose up in rebellion against their Creator; instantly they were hurled from the highest heaven into the deepest hell; from angels they were transformed into demons; and Lucifer, the brightest spirit in heaven, became the foulest, the most hideous monster of perdition. Adam was created, and constituted in the state of original justice, but scarcely had he yielded to the solicitations of Eve, and thus offended God, when he was struck by Divine malediction, and afflicted with innumerable misfortunes in body and soul. The men who lived before the deluge, forgetting the justice of God, the chastiser of sin, and disregarding reason, surrendered themselves to the gratification of their animal appetites, and God, in the fury of his wrath, opening the flood-gates of heaven, and breaking up the fountains of the great deep (*Gen.* vii. 11), submerged in the waters of the deluge all living creatures on the face of the earth. Sodom and Gomorrha sinned, and the Lord rained down brimstone and fire out of heaven, and consumed those wicked cities with the whole country round about, and all the inhabitants (*Gen.* xix. 25). The Israelites sinned in the desert, and out of six hundred thousand men fit to bear arms, Josue and Caleb alone arrived safe at the land of promise (*Numb.* xiv. 30). What are we, then, to do, who so easily fall into sin? Who will defend us against the rigor of God's justice? The Fathers reply, that Mary is our advocate, and an advocate so powerful that she can save us all.

Mary most certainly loved us with exceeding great love. Of this she gave evident proof when she consented to the Incarnation of the Divine Word, that the human race might be rescued from the evils occasioned by sin. The accomplishment of the glorious mystery of the Incarnation depended on the answer of Mary to the Angel Gabriel, and in the eternal decrees of the Almighty, one of the requisite conditions for the Incarnation was free and full consent of Mary. This is the essential obligation under which we lie to the Queen of Virgins; for it is a point of faith that, through her, Christ has been given to us, and that to her we are indebted for a Savior. If the Son of God descended from heaven to earth—if, in the most pure bosom of Mary, he was made man for the salvation of man, this was done the very instant she said, and because she said, Behold the handmaid of the Lord; be it done to me according to Thy word. The Blessed Virgin did not redeem us, nor did she, in the strictest sense merit anything for us; still by impetration, by merit in a wide sense, and by contributing by her consent to the Incarnation of the Word, she coöperated in some manner in our redemption. Mary, says St. Antoninus, gave birth, for us, to him who created anew or regenerated us all by his passion. The Lord, says Richard of St. Lawrence (*c* i. *de Laud. V.*), was with Mary, and Mary was with the Lord in the same labor, and the same work of our redemption. The Mother of Mercy aided the Father of mercies in the work of our salvation. The Lord said of Adam: It is not good for man to be alone ; let us make him a help like unto himself (*Gen.* ii. 18). But Eve was of no help to Adam ; she was the cause of his destruction. But this new Eve was of help; she is the Jahal into whose hands Sisara was delivered; she is the Judith who threw into confusion the house of Nabuchodonosor. Mary, therefore, may be justly said to have coöperated in the redemption of man.

Another great proof of the protection of Mary is deduced from what is recorded in holy Gospels as having occurred when man's redemption was on the point of being consummated. The Savior was about to expire on the cross, a victim for the salvation of all mankind. He was racked by the severest sufferings. Mary and John, at the foot of the cross, tasted the bitterness of his passion. The dying Jesus opens his eyes, and beholds his tender mother and his beloved disciple, weighed down with sorrow on his account. He feels compassion for them, and reflecting that the mother remains deprived of her Son and the disciple of his master, he wishes to console them. He says to his mother: In John behold thy son; and to John, In Mary behold thy mother—Woman, behold thy son. After that he saith to the disciple, Behold thy mother (*John* xix. 26). These words increase the affliction of Mary, but she penetrates their mysterious sense, and kindly accepts the charge imposed upon her—a charge full of consolation for us. We were born again into life under the saving wood of the cross, as we have incurred death under the tree of sin. We see, therefore, that our Redeemer having us all before his eyes in his beloved disciple, and aiming at naught by his passion but our welfare, wished us to possess a mother in Mary, and a loving and powerful mother.

If Mary coöperated in our redemption, if she is the mother of God, and if Jesus Christ committed us to her charge, as her children of adoption, we have many and weighty titles of confidence in her patronage. Christ was our Redeemer, because, to liberate us from the slavery of Satan, he took upon himself human flesh, and died for our salvation, but being a priest forever he is able also to save forever them that come unto God by himself; always living to make intercession for us (*Heb.* vii. 25). Mary likewise lives in heaven, and still discharges the office of our mediatrix. If you fear, says St. Bernard to the sinner (*Serm. de Aquoed.*), if you fear to approach the Father, he has given you Jesus as a mediator; if you desire an advocate before Jesus, have recourse to Mary. If our adversary and accuser, the devil, says Gerson, endeavors to crush us in any way, we possess in Mary a most kind patroness, a most wise advocate, and a most powerful ally, proclaimed by the whole Church the Queen of Mercy and our protectress. Who, exclaims a holy servant of Mary, who after Christ is more watchful over the welfare of the human race, than thou art? Who shields us in our afflictions, if thou dost not ? Who furnishes us with the assistance, and delivers us from temptation? Who, by prayer and supplication, combats more strenuously in favor of sinners? No one obtains salvation, unless through thee, O Virgin most holy! No one escapes from evils, unless through thy patronage, O Virgin most pure !

Mary is, moreover, a most powerful advocate, because she is the mother of Jesus. He, although in virtue of the hypostatic union with the person of the Lord, enjoys supreme dominion over all men and also over Mary; as long as he remained on earth he was subject to her as his mother. Hence, according to St. Bonaventure and St. Peter Damian, she possesses even now, with her Son, the power to obtain for us whatsoever she wishes, and to excite to hope of salvation the most obdurate and abandoned. Mary, while on earth, consoled the spouses of Cana when wine failed them; will she neglect to console the faithful, that they may be strengthened for the acquisition of heaven? Mary has obtained from her Son many temporal favors; will she not obtain for us spiritual blessings? The Virgin, says the Angelic Doctor, holds one half of the authority of heaven; she is the Queen of Mercy; to her Son is reserved the empire of justice.

II.

Her power to give assistance, and lead to salvation, Mary exercises in an especial manner in favor of sinners. She has been appointed our mother by the Redeemer, and we are her children by adoption. If a son is attacked by disease, or cast into prison, his mother watches by his side night and day, until his health is re-established, or spares no exertions to effect his liberation. Mary acts in the same manner towards sinners. When a man falls into sin, he loses the grace of God; he loses all merit; he grows feeble in spirit, and of his own will stretches forth his hands to receive the manacles of the enemy of God. The sinner does not perceive his own miserable state; he does not understand that in renouncing heaven he is rushing headlong into an immense ocean of torments in the regions of eternal woe. Mary feels compassion for him; she never loses sight of him; on the part of God she stings his heart with remorse; she obtains light for his mind, and inclinations to repentance for his will; and she never ceases to pray and supplicate, until she sees him loosed from the bonds of sin, and restored to the life of grace. The interposition of the angels and saints is powerful in behalf of sinners; but much more powerful is that of Mary, for she recruited a number of angels diminished by the rebellion, and reconciled human nature with Almighty God, by giving birth to Jesus Christ. How many would be lost forever, how many would remain in their blindness, and precipitate into the abyss in desperation, were it not for the influence of the Blessed Virgin with her Son! Mary is a wall of defense for those who have recourse to her, and her mercy is a power of refuge. Mary was prefigured in the ark of Noe, which furnished protection not only to the family of Noe but also to irrational animals. Under the mantle of Mary, not only the just find shelter, but sinners also, who by their vices have degraded themselves to the level of brutes. Mary is the dove of Noe, bearing a branch of olives in sign of the peace which the Almighty grants to men. Mary is the kind Rebecca, who gave to drink not only to the servant of Abraham but also to his camel. Mary is the prudent Abigail who appeases the anger of David and restrained him from revenge. Mary, by her entreaties, frequently restrains the avenging arm of God, already lifted to strike, and obtains for sinners a return to grace, and the happy lot of becoming children of God instead of children of wrath. The rainbow round about the throne of God, which was seen by St. John (*Apoc.* iv. 3), was also a figure of Mary; she is ever present before the throne, to mitigate the severity of sinners. After the deluge, the Lord said to Noe: This is the sign of the covenant which I give between me and you: I will set my bow in the clouds, and it shall be the sign of a covenant between me and between the earth: and I shall see it, and shall remember the everlasting covenant (*Gen.* ix. 12). The Fathers teach us that Mary is this bow of everlasting peace. When the prayers of Mary ascend before the presence of God, he grants to sinners the redemption of their sins, and forms with them an alliance of friendship. We may, therefore, conclude with St. Anselm, that Mary was made the mother of God more for sinners than for the just, as Christ came to call not the just, but sinners.

ASPIRATION.

From God's anger protect us, holy Virgin Mary.

PRACTICE.

Implore frequently the protection of the Blessed Virgin.

LITANY.

Read the Ave Maria.

TWENTY-SECOND DAY.

MARY, MOTHER OF SUCCOR AND COMPAS-SION.

"When Michol, David's wife, had told him this, she let him down through the window, and he escaped." 1 *Kings* xix. 11.

SAUL, filled with envy, persecuted David and sought his death. He on one occasion endeavored to nail David to the wall with his spear, but the spear missed him and David fled and escaped that night. Saul, therefore, sent his guards to David's house to watch him that he might be killed in the morning (1 *Kings* xix. 10). But the faithful Michol, having been informed of the designs of the envious king against her innocent husband, said to David: Unless thou save thyself this night, to-morrow thou wilt die. She let him down through a window during the darkness of the night, and he fled and took refuge with Samuel in Najoth of Ramatha. Michol was a figure of Mary; but Michol's one act of beneficence was confined to David, whereas, Mary's acts of beneficence are without number and extend their influence to the whole human race. Lucifer still retains his envious malice, and endeavors to satisfy it by dragging the creatures of God along with himself into eternal torments. He watches with great sagacity, and takes advantage of the circumstances favorable to an attack; he at one time makes open war upon man, and at another endeavors to circumvent him by hidden approaches. The just man he strives to despoil of his justice; the sinner he labors to involve more thoroughly in sin and lead to utter desperation. The life of man on earth thus becomes a continual warfare (*Job.* vii. 1). What is man to do? What angel will guard him ? Where shall he find a harbor of salvation? The Church replies: Mary, O sinner, is thy guardian angel; Mary is thy port of refuge; Mary is thy Michol. Mary compassionates us in our misfortunes and is a mother of succor and compassion, for the just that they may persevere, for sinners that they may repent and do penance for their sins.

I.

Man is made just by sanctifying grace. Grace is a divine gift, a supernatural quality, infused into the soul by the Almighty, which, purifying the soul from the stains of sin and rendering it acceptable to the Most High, makes us children of God and heirs of the kingdom of heaven. With grace are united the infused virtues and the gifts of the Holy Ghost. But every thing in the spiritual life depends upon sanctifying grace. For, as the soul by means of its natural faculties produces its operations, so sanctifying grace by means of the infused virtues and spiritual gifts accomplishes its supernatural works. The just man lives and operates by faith, hope, charity, and other virtues; just as the soul has knowledge of things by means of the understanding, recalls the past by means of the memory, and determines its operations by the will. As the soul is the principle and cause of natural life, grace is the principle and cause of supernatural life. The soul is never deprived of its natural faculties and grace is never without its virtues and supernatural gifts. They are inseparable from it.

It is easy now to understand how highly sanctifying grace should be esteemed and how diligently it should be guarded. Grace is a treasure laid up in the soul, but we carry this treasure in earthen vessels. We are in danger of being robbed of it by powerful enemies, such as the world, the devil, and the flesh. God without being asked grants many graces; but these are, for the most part, of ordinary character. He has not promised to grant extraordinary graces unless to those who beg them earnestly. This is the common opinion of theologians, and it seems indicated in the words of Christ. Watch ye, therefore, praying at all times that you may be accounted worthy to escape all these things that are to come, and to stand before the Son of man (*Luke* xxi. 36). All men need an especial grace to be able to persevere in the friendship of God to the very last instant of life; and one of the principal means assigned by God for obtaining this grace is prayer. After a man has been justified by grace, says St. Thomas (i. 2. q. 109; a. 10.), it is necessary for him to beg of God the gift of perseverance, that he may be preserved from sin to the end of his days. For to many grace is given to whom it is not given to persevere in grace. St. James, writing to all the faithful, says: If any of you want wisdom let him ask of God, who giveth to all abundantly, and upbraideth not, and it shall be given to him (i. 5). If we are truly devout to Mary, we shall be able to preserve the treasure of grace and obtain final perseverance; for, in the opinion of the Fathers, all the graces which God bestows on us pass through the hands of Mary.

The Church calls the Blessed Virgin our life and our hope. Therefore, with her intercession, we maintain ourselves in grace and all reach heaven. The Church itself represents Mary as uttering the following words: I made that in the heavens there should rise light that never faileth; and as a cloud I covered all the earth. I am the Mother of fair love, and of fear, and of knowledge, and of holy hope. In me is all grace of the way and of the truth; in me is all hope of life and of virtue. Come over to me, all ye that desire me, and be filled with my fruits; for my spirit is sweet above honey and the honeycomb. My memory is unto everlasting generations. He that hearkeneth to me shall not be confounded, and they that work by me shall not sin (*Eccl.* xxiv.). To preserve ourselves in grace, spiritual fortitude in resisting all our enemies is necessary, and the gifts of God are indispensable. But we acquire all that is requisite by having recourse to Mary. She thus continues to address us: O ye men, to you I call, and my voice is to the sons of men. Counsel and equity are mine; prudence is mine; strength is mine. By me kings reign, and lawgivers decree just things. By me princes rule, and the mighty decree justice. With me are riches and glory, glorious riches and justice. For my fruit is better than gold and the precious stones, and my blossoms than choice silver. I walk in the way of justice, in the midst of the paths of judgment, that I may enrich them that love me and fill their treasures (*Prov.* viii.). As the Church and the Fathers particularly refer to Mary in a mystical sense all that is contained in the books of Proverbs and of Ecclesiasticus, it is apparent how the faithful on the earth by means of Mary govern their senses and passions, so as to be able to persevere to the end and secure eternal happiness.

Mary, not without mystic meaning, is likened to the fairest and most elegant objects in nature. She is compared to the cedar because by her beneficent influence she puts to flight the infernal serpent; to the cypress, because she inspires the fragrance of holiness and saintly repute; to the palm, because she makes us victorious over ourselves; to the vine, because she leads us to produce fruits of heavenly virtues; to the olive, because she brings peace to the soul; to oil, to signify the grace which she obtains for us from God; to the plane tree, because she defends us against our passions; to the rose, on account of the divine love which she excites in our hearts; to the lily, because she breathes purity into the soul; and to nard, because she invests Christian humility with sweetness. Mary, as the dawn, sends down the first rays of light to the sinner for his conversion; as the sun, she guides us along the pathway of life; as the moon, she enlightens us in darkness of spirit resulting from human weakness; as a star, she conducts us safely to the harbor of paradise. The Holy Virgin even on earth was always prompt to offer relief to the afflicted and unfortunate, and we know that she enjoyed the privilege of having all her requests complied with. At the marriage at Cana of Galilee, when the wine failed, she said to Jesus, They have no wine (*John* ii. 3). And Jesus said to her: Woman, what is that to me and thee? My hour is not yet come. Although Jesus seemed to refuse to perform a miracle, she said with confidence to the waiters: Whatsoever he shall say to you, do ye. And Jesus finally converted water into wine. Although the Redeemer, says St. Thomas, had determined to perform no miracle until his public life should commence, he yielded to the request of his mother, and out of regard for her, wrought the first of his wonders.

All the saints of heaven enjoy from God a certain right of patronage, in virtue of which they can render assistance to those who apply to themselves; but the Blessed Virgin, being queen of saints and angels, possesses from God a most extraordinary power by which she is the patroness and advocate of all men. And the more faithfully and sincerely she is honored by men, the more actively is her patronage called forth in their favor. She is not only the servant of God's predilection and his fondly cherished daughter, but she is the mother of God himself and the spouse of the Holy Ghost. No other creature can obtain from God the graces which Mary, mother of God, can obtain for her servants in their necessities. One sigh of Mary's is more potent than the suffrages of all the saints. Mary is therefore for the just man a mother of succor and compassion, through whom he is enabled to persevere in the grace mercifully bestowed by Almighty God.

II.

Mary gives succor to sinners to enable them to rise from the unhappy state of sin. The sinner is in a most deplorable condition. He lives, indeed, an animal life, but is utterly destitute of spiritual life. He may be compared to a blind man, who, if he has not some one to lead him constantly by the hand, goes groping about, in danger every moment of falling into a pit or down a precipice. He may also be compared to the idols of the Gentiles, which, says the Psalmist (*Ps.* cxv.), have eyes and see not, ears and hear not, mouths and speak not, hands and feel not, feet and walk not. The sinner has eyes and sees not, because in the darkness which surrounds him he cannot distinguish truth from falsehood; he has ears and hears not, because he either does not listen to the word of God, or, if he listens to it, having his mind crowded with earthly thoughts he occupies himself with these alone; he has a tongue and tastes not, because, habituated to the corruption of vile pleasure, he finds no relish in virtue; he has hands, but he applies them not to works of salvation; he has feet, but instead of walking in the way of righteousness, he rushes headlong into the vortex of crimes. To be able to act, the blind man wants light, and the idol, life. The sinner, in like manner, lying helpless in the darkness of his iniquities, in order to rise from his unhappy condition and perform works of spiritual life, requires the light and aid of the grace of God.

But Mary is the refuge of sinners. Before the birth of Mary, says Richard of St. Lawrence, we had none to be our advocate with the divine Word. But God the Father said: It is not good for man to be alone, let us give him a help, and let this help be the Blessed Virgin. She shall be a mediatrix for the human race in the presence of my Son, as my Son shall be a mediator in presence of myself. Mary is the mother of grace, and the sinner who seeks after her finds grace and salvation. He that shall find me shall find life, and shall have salvation from the Lord (*Prov.* vii. 35).

Whilst the Israelites were passing through the desert, they were protected from the burning heat of the sun by a miraculous cloud which the Almighty caused to appear in the heavens. Thus Mary, say the Fathers, like an intervening cloud, shelters sinners from the anger of God and the fury of temptations. We may approach God with security whilst the Mother is in presence of the Son and the Son in presence of the Father. Mary reminds the Son of the motherly solicitude with which she watched over him, of her anxieties, her fears, on his account, of the toils, the privations, which he endured; the Son exhibits to the Father his wounds, his head crowned with thorns, the cross on which he poured forth his life. Can the Son reject the appeals of Mary ? Can the Father look with indifference on the Lamb that was slain in his honor? Let us therefore conclude with St. Anselm (*de Excl. V.* ii. 1), if for the sake of sinners Mary was made the mother of God, how can any enormity of sin cause us to despair of pardon?

ASPIRATION.

Turn away my eyes, O Lord, that they may not behold vanity; quicken me in thy way (*Ps.* cxviii. 37).

PRACTICE.

Receive every trial with patience, in honor of Jesus and Mary.

LITANY.

Read "Chats About the Rosary."

TWENTY-THIRD DAY.

PATRONAGE OF MARY.

''The Lord hath blessed thee by his power, because by thee he hath brought our enemies to naught.'' *Judith* xiii. 22.

FULL of anger and indignation, Holofernes closely besieged Bethulia. Every thing portended the approaching fall of that unfortunate city. The citizens were in a state of extreme destitution, perishing of hunger and thirst. Heaven seemed deaf to their prayers. Then all gathering themselves together to Ozias, all together with one voice, said: There is no one to help us, while we are cast down before the eyes of our enemies in thirst, and great destruction. And now assemble ye all that are in the city, that we may of our own accord yield ourselves all up to Holofernes; for it is better, that being captives we should live and bless the Lord, than that we should die and be a reproach to all flesh(*Judith* vii. 14). When Judith heard that Ozias had promised that he would deliver up the city after the fifth day, she sent for the ancients, and said to them: Who are you that tempt the Lord? You have set a time for the mercy of the Lord, and you have appointed him a day according to your pleasure (*Judith* vii. 11). I have formed a plan for the liberation of our city, but I desire that you search not into what I am doing. Pray only that God may strengthen my design. She then went forth to combat the enemies of her country with no other arms than those of fasting, prayer, beauty, courage, and holy confidence in God. Judith cut off the head of Holofernes, and the Assyrian army was broken, put to flight, and dispersed. Bethulia was delivered, and Judith was celebrated as its saviour. Thou, exclaimed the high priest and the ancients, thou art the glory of Jerusalem; thou art the joy of Israel; thou art the honor of our people (*Judith* xv. 10). Interpreting allegorically with the Fathers this historical fact, Holofernes is Satan; the Bethulians, the people of God; and Judith, Mary our protectress. We live indeed in a world of peril; and our adversary, the devil, as a roaring lion goeth about seeking whom he may devour (*I. Pet.* v. 8). But take courage, children of God; as Judith delivered the Bethulians, so will Mary deliver us from the fangs of the infernal dragon and all his temptations, if we honor her with true, sincere, heartfelt devotion. Let us consider now the virtue of Mary's patronage, in the assaults and temptations of the enemy during life and at the moment of death. But let us begin by addressing Mary in the words said to Judith after her return from the Assyrian camp: The Lord hath blessed thee by his power, because by thee he hath brought our enemies to naught.

I.

Almighty God when he created man, in his goodness and mercy destined him for heaven; but scarcely had man been formed when the decree of death was promulgated against him. Man is no sooner born than he begins to send forth cries of distress; he has already taken possession of the inheritance bequeathed us by our first father, an inheritance of woes and miseries which we can never alienate on earth. Man is born, but at his birth he bears in his bosom the germ of death. Pains, sorrows, infirmities, wear his system every day, and lead him on insensibly to the grave. We are dying every day. But far more lamentable is the detriment to the soul and its danger. By the sin of Adam a frightful revolution was caused in the soul of man, with vast prejudice to its faculties, the memory was enfeebled, the intellect obscured, and the will rendered prone to evil. Reason lost its rectitude, and the germ of tumultuous passions was introduced into the heart. Experience teaches that with the development of the members and the increase of years the passions are developed and grow in power. The imagination and thought of man's heart are prone to evil from his youth (*Gen.* viii. 21). But who could describe the evils which surround man and conspire against his spiritual life on earth and happiness in heaven? The combats and wars which rage in his bosom? Who could number the enemies who have sworn his destruction? The leaves of the forest are not equal in multitude to the ills with which man is afflicted; not so boisterous is the storm-tossed ocean as the heart of man stirred up by his passions. St. John assures us that all that is in the world is the concupiscence of the flesh, and the concupiscence of the eyes, and the pride of life (1 *John* ii. 16). On the other hand, our wrestling is not against flesh and blood, but against principalities and powers, against the rulers of the world of this darkness; against the spirits of wickedness in the high places (*Eph.* vi. 12). If we consider our mind, we find it frequently clouded by the fumes of vanity, of honors, and of ambition; if we consider our heart, we find it boiling with furious passions, its affections vicious, inclined to pride, avarice, impurity, and anger; and if we consider the actions of man, we find that they are too often works of darkness and sin. All this chiefly arises from the cunning of Satan, who is incessantly striving by his temptations to lead us into evil.   Unhappy that we are! Who shall deliver us from the body of this death, and from the temptations which assail us at every moment and seek to make us slaves to the law of sin? The grace of God by Jesus Christ our Lord, and the most glorious Virgin, will be our deliverers (*Rom.* vii. 23-25).

After God, Mary is our great advocate and our deliverer from the temptations which cause us so much annoyance and so greatly endanger our souls. The motherhood of Mary elevated her to a dignity so sublime, that the Angelic Doctor calls it almost infinite; because a creature cannot be more intimately united with God than by being his mother (1 *p. q.* 25. *a.* 6).   In the opinion of some doctors, Mary obtained the title of Mediatrix, not by her merits, nor by having prayed for the salvation of men, nor by having given birth to Jesus, but by having freely and willingly offered her Son to the death of the cross to deliver us from the slavery of Satan and sin. Mary, says St. Epiphanius, discharged the office of priest and altar. In the temple, she offered her Son in sacrifice, holding him in her arms; on Golgotha she confirmed the offering already made, and on the altar of her heart she consumed that great holocaust of love with the excess of her patience and charity. There were two altars on Calvary; one in the body of Christ, the other in the bosom of Mary. Christ immolated his flesh, Mary her heart, for the benefit of sinners. With this title of Mediatrix, Mary received almost unlimited authority, in virtue of which she is queen of heaven and earth, and of hell also, defeated by her virtues. Although she is now enjoying the glory of heaven, she is not forgetful of us; she understands more distinctly now our afflictions and our struggles of soul, and she is more solicitous and expeditious in lending us succor.

This daily struggle of ours, and the protection which we have in Mary, was symbolically foretold by the Almighty in the beginning of the world. When Adam and Eve were created and ennobled with

sanctifying grace, God commanded them
not to eat of the fruit of the tree of knowledge of good and evil, and made death
the penalty of disobedience. Satan, des-
perate in his own fall and filled with
vengeful feelings against God himself,
could not suffer patiently that Adam and
Eve should be more faithful to God in
Eden than he had been in heaven. He
called into action against them all his
powers of cunning; and so successfully,
that he induced them to transgress the
command of God. The Lord in his mercy
promised them a Redeemer, and said to
the serpent: I will put enmities between
thee and the woman, and thy seed and
her seed; she shall crush thy head (*Gen.*
xiii. 15). Who is this great woman of
promise if it is not Mary, who, by giving
birth to Christ, and by her holy life, conquered the serpent of the infernal abyss?
The Fathers unanimously recognize, as
promised in that woman, Mary, the
Mother of Jesus. She shall crush thy head.
Some refer these words immediately to
Christ, on the authority of the reading of
some versions: He shall crush thy head.
But this difference of reading is of slight
importance; it is certain that Christ has
discomfited Lucifer, but he has done it in
the body taken from Mary, so that Mary

has really, by means of her Son, crushed the head of the serpent, and she still rests her foot upon his prostrate form.

But Satan, though conquered, still spreads terror throughout the world, still meditates our ruin, and nurses vengeance in his heart. He lies in wait for the innocent, and watches his opportunity to overwhelm them. Like a hungry lion he catches the slightest sound of approaching prey ; he steals upon his unsuspecting victim, and with a sudden spring bears him to the ground. He passes over the earth as a cloud pregnant with the storm passes along the heavens. It moves slowly at first and excites little apprehension; it gradually assumes a dangerous aspect; then, all at once, it darts forth its lightnings and unchains all its thunderbolts. But happy are we, if we honor Mary as a mother. Mothers are unwilling to lose sight of their children; Mary, then, will keep her eyes upon her servants, and not suffer them to be deceived by the cunning or overthrown by the power of Lucifer.

When the Israelites were about to undertake a war or engage in battle with some enemy, they immediately turned their eyes to the ark. From it they derived strength for their arms and courage for their souls; and by means of it they came off victorious. When the ark was lifted up, Moses said: Arise, O Lord, and let thy enemies be scattered, and let them that hate thee flee from before thy face (*Numb.* iv. 35). In this manner Moses overcame the nations that opposed his passage. The city of Jericho was not taken till the ark was borne seven times around the walls; and whilst it was borne round for the seventh time, the walls fell of themselves, and the Israelites entered and took possession of the city (*Jos.* vi.). The ark was a figure of Mary. The ark containing the manna, says Cornelius à Lapide, is the Blessed Virgin, who supplies man with strength to oppose the devil. In the patronage of Mary, therefore, we find power against the temptations which assail us.

II.

Death is terrible to all; even the greatest saints dreaded it. Various reasons produce fear of death, but let us here dwell upon two alone: the uncertainty of our future lot, and the temptations with which the devil usually assaults us in our last moments. Then, in the silence of the passions, all other thoughts are rejected; those thoughts alone occupy us which regard the life to come. The consciousness that time is drawing to a close causes the dying man to reflect seriously upon his own soul, upon God, and eternity, but the devil then comes down to us, having great wrath, knowing that he hath but a short time (*Apoc.* xii. 12). He is tortured with envy at the thought that we, aided by divine grace, shall take possession of seats once intended for him and his followers and he employs all his knowledge and puts in practice all his arts in order to gain us as companions in the dwelling place of eternal woe. The dying Christian groans in agony of spirit, and after God, finds no resource except the protection of Mary.

St. Bonaventure teaches us that Mary sends to her dying servants St. Michael and other celestial spirits, to defend them against the temptations of the enemy, and to meet the souls of those who were particularly devout to her and conduct them in triumph to heaven. Lucifer, on the contrary, stirs up the lowest regions of ruin, and despatches his most cruel ministers to watch the dying man, and tear, if possible, his soul from the bosom of God. But the merciful God, says St. Germanus, has given such power to Mary that the malignant spirits fly in dismay at her very beck, and would rather undergo any increase of torture than see themselves swayed by the authority of Mary. Who then will be so bold as to accuse before the Supreme Judge him whom Mary patronizes? Mary herself visits her devout servants at the last hour, and bears to them strength and encouragement and consolation. What a happiness to have Mary for a protectress in death!

ASPIRATION.

Show thyself a Mother, most amiable Virgin.

PRACTICE.

Be careful to avoid every occasion of sin.

LITANY.

Read Alban Butler on the feasts of the Blessed Virgin.

TWENTY-FOURTH DAY.

PROTECTION OF MARY.

"He conducted them with a cloud by day, and all the night with a light of fire." *Ps.* lxxii. 14.

THE Hebrews had withdrawn themselves from the yoke of Egyptian servitude; they had passed the Red Sea, treading its sands with unmoistened feet; they had seen, at the stretching forth of the hand of Moses, the waters of the deep reunite themselves, and shut up in the middle of the waves Pharao and his whole army—his foot soldiers, his chariots and his horsemen; and Moses and the children of Israel had sung that admirable canticle of exultation, in which are manifested the mercies of God with his people. Suddenly the Israelites are seized with terror, feeling themselves imprisoned in that vast wilderness. Behind them was the sea like an interminable wall; before them, the desert without boundary. And although they were miraculously provided with food by the Almighty, during the day they were without shelter from the rays of the burning sun, and at night were in darkness without guidance for their footsteps. But the Lord did not neglect them in their necessities. He caused a wonderful cloud to appear in the sky, which afforded them shade by day, and at night, glowing like fire, shed light round on every side. It also assumed the form of a pillar, and served to direct them in their wanderings. The pillar of the cloud by day, and the pillar of the fire by night, never failed as long as Israel remained in the wilderness. The Fathers teach that in the pillar of cloud was prefigured the Holy Virgin, and as it served for guidance and pro-tection to the children of Israel, so Mary guides her servants safely through the darksome paths of life, and defends them against the unceasing attacks of their enemies. Mary, says St. Bonaventure, delivers us from the fury of the indigna-tion of God, and the power of the tempt-ation of Satan. Let us now consider that Mary displays the virtue of her protection, in preserving her devout servants from the pains of hell, and in liberating them from the flames of Pur-gatory.

I.

How terrible is the thought of Hell! The torments of that place of horror are innumerable; but to two, principally, they

are reduced by theologians, to the penalty
of loss and the penalty of sense—*pœna
damni* and *pœna sensus*. The penalty of
loss consists in the privation of the vision
of God, in which is found eternal beatitude; the penalty of sense consists in the
sensible sufferings with which the lost
ones are tortured. By the penalty of loss
the reprobate is excluded from his last
end, can never see the face of God, can never raise his eyes to heaven, and is deprived
of every good. He is forever the enemy
of God, an object of his hatred and vengeance; and God, so to speak, casts him
off as if he were no longer his creature.
Hence arises an extreme, irreconcilable,
and mutual hatred between God and the
sinner. As to the penalty of the sense, no
eloquence could portray its frightfulness.
All that can be expressed is far below the
truth. All the afflictions ever endured
by the unfortunate, all the cruelties exercised on the martyrs, afford only
a feeble idea of the torments of the
damned. Our material fire, the very
touch of which causes inexpressible pain,
is but a shadow of that devouring fire,
which every moment produces death-ag-
onies that never end in death.

Some conception of the dreadfulness of
those tortures may be drawn from the re-

flection that they are eternal, and are inflicted by an infinite, an Almighty God, infinitely outraged by the sinner. Men and women, old and young, all who die impenitent, are confusedly heaped together in that abode of horror. It was created in the beginning for Lucifer and his rebel associates, but it opened its gates to man after the sin of Adam. There are to be seen piled upon one another, pagans, idolaters, jews, mahometans, heretics and schismatics, and amongst them many with the sign of salvation upon their brows, who forfeited the claims which it gave them; Catholics, but forsworn Catholics, still bearing the mark of faith which they dishonored, but only for their never ending shame. And many are called but few are chosen. Great God! who can escape thy anger? How avoid thy fury? How shall we be able to resist rebellious concupiscence, evil examples, perverse inclinations, and the rulers of the world of this darkness?

We are indeed navigating a tempestuous sea filled with hidden rocks; but our star shines forth and points out the harbor of salvation. If our passions entice us out of the way, and leave us wandering like bewildered travelers, Mary causes a ray of light from on high to flash across our minds, which reconducts our footsteps to the right path; and thus she delivers us from hell, into which we were rushing by our sins. Mary delivers no one who is actually lost, for in hell there is no redemption. But whoever commits mortal sin, is from that moment a victim of perdition. If Mary, by her intercession, enlightens his mind, and touches his heart, and recalls him to the life of grace, she may be said to deliver him from eternal ruin, because she rescues him from that condition which would inevitably precipitate him into everlasting flames. Nor is Mary the deliverer of those who, relying on their imaginary devotion to her, sin with less hesitation. Their presumption deserves punishment, not protection. But the sinner who wishes sincerely to change his life, and recommends himself earnestly to the mother of God, shall surely discover that Mary is also the sinner's mother, and she will rescue him from destruction. There is nothing so good that men may not misuse it; they abuse even the goodness of God. But human malice cannot affect the nature of holiness and truth. We need not, therefore, hesitate to proclaim that it is morally impossible for that sinner to be lost who, truly penitent for his sins, practises devotion to the Virgin Mary.

The titles with which the Church honors Mary, show the exceeding esteem in which it holds her influence. It extols her as the mother of grace and of mercy; as defence against our enemy—our advocate and mediatrix. The Holy Fathers are unanimous in celebrating the power of Mary's protection. St. Ignatius, Martyr, proclaims: It is impossible for the sinner to be saved, unless through the help and favor of the Holy Virgin. Those whom the justice of God does not save, Mary saves, in her boundless mercy, by the unlimited virtue of her intercession. St. Antoninus writes (*p.* 4, *tit.* 50): As it is impossible for those to obtain salvation from whom Mary withdraws her eyes of mercy, so it becomes, in a certain manner, necessary that those on whom she looks with kindness, interceding in their behalf, reach the haven of happiness and be glorified forever in paradise. St. Anselm teaches (*de Excel. v. c.* ii.), that, as it is impossible for one who is not favored by her, to attain eternal life, so it is impossible that he be lost who recurs to her with confidence, and is regarded by her with affection. St. Bernard, asking the reason why the Church invokes Mary as the queen and mother of mercy, replies: Because she is believed to open the treasures of divine mercy to whom she pleases and as she pleases, so that no sinner, however enormous his crimes, perishes, in whose behalf the queen of saints interposes with God.

The Church applies to Mary the words of the book of Proverbs, All that hate me love death (xxiv. 36). And those of Ecclesiasticus, He that hearkeneth to me shall not be confounded (xxiv. 30). Mary is the valiant woman of scripture, who, like the merchant's ship, bringeth her bread from afar (*Prov.* xxxi. 14). In the stormy ocean of this world all are shipwrecked who do not seek refuge on board this vessel. Mary is the tower of strength, that defends all who take shelter in it against the most violent assaults of their enemies. Mary is the ark of safety, which buoys us up amidst raging billows, and prevents us from being ingulfed in the abyss. Mary is the effulgent sun which irradiates our intellect, so that we open our eyes to divine grace and abandon the life of sin. Let us therefore conclude, with the words of St. John of Damascus, O great mother of God, if I repose my confidence in thee, I shall be saved. If I place myself under thy protection, I have nothing to fear; for devotion to thee is a means of salvation which God grants to those alone whom he wishes to bless forever (*Serm. de B. V.*).

II.

After having considered that the protection of Mary preserves sinners from hell, let us consider her great solicitude for the deliverance of the souls in purgatory. Although those souls are inexpressibly dear to Almighty God, still, as nothing soiled can enter the kingdom of heaven, and as they passed from this life with some sin not atoned for, Divine Justice demands that they should make expiation in the painful prison of purgatory. In the opinion of the Fathers, the sufferings of the souls in purgatory are excessively intense. St. Augustine says that the fire of purgatory is more severely tormenting than all the punishments and afflictions that can be seen, felt, or conceived in this world. It is the sentiment of St. Thomas, with theologians commonly, that the fire of purgatory has the same power as the fire of hell. In hell the soul is tortured by eternal flames; in purgatory these same flames torture for the limited time appointed by Divine Justice.The fire of purgatory,by supernatural power, operates immediately upon the soul,and necessarily causes far greater suffering in the soul than ordinary fire could cause by its action on the body.

Mary assuages the sufferings of the souls in purgatory. She said to St. Bridget: I am the loving mother of all the souls detained in purgatory; because the punishment which they endure for their sins is constantly mitigated, in some measure, through my prayers. The Blessed Virgin, says St. Bernardine of Siena, extends her dominion over the kingdom of purgatory, and by the authority which she derives from her dignity, her merits, and her prayers, delivers her devout servants from their prison of torment (*Ac.* ii. *c.*3, *de Nom. M.*). The name of Mary to the souls in purgatory is a name of encouragement and consolation, and her prayers are like the shower of a summer cloud, which refreshes the heated atmosphere and revives the languid and drooping flowers of the garden. And not only are the sufferings of purgatory mitigated by the merits and prayers of Mary, but their duration is abbreviated (*Novarinus.*). Mary's protection,therefore, softens the pains of purgatory, and obtains deliverance from its flames, and, moreover, prevents sinners from falling into perdition by leading them to repentance and reformation of life.

ASPIRATION.

From sudden and unprovided death deliver us, O Holy Virgin.

PRACTICE.

Ask the protection and blessing of Mary before every important action.

LITANY.

Read The B. V. M. in the Gospels.

TWENTY-FIFTH DAY.

MARY OUR HOPE.

"Go in, thou and all thy house, into the ark."
Gen. ii. 1.

At the time of Noe, men and their sins had been greatly multiplied. The different parts of the world were crowded with lovers of ease and gratifications. Their thoughts and language, we may well suppose, were similar to those of the impious in the book of Wisdom. The time of our life is short and tedious;we are born of nothing, and after this we shall be as if we had not been. After this life our body shall be ashes, and our spirit shall be poured abroad as soft air, and our life shall pass away as the trace of a cloud, and shall be dispersed as a mist which is driven away by the beams of the sun and overpowered with the heat thereof. Our time is as the passing of a shadow, and there is no going back of our end. Come, therefore, and let us enjoy the good things that are present. Let us crown ourselves with roses before they be withered; let no meadow escape our riot; let us everywhere leave tokens of joy for this our portion and this our lot (*Wisd.* ii.). Almighty God, seeing that the wickedness of men was great on earth, and hearing the blasphemies of their impiety, it repented him that he had made man; and being touched inwardly with sorrow of heart, he said: I will destroy man whom I have created from the face of the earth,—from man even to beasts, from the creeping thing even to the fowls of the air— for it repenteth me that I have made them. And he said to Noe: The end of all flesh is come before me, the earth is filled with iniquity through them and I will destroy them with the earth. Make thee an ark of timber planks to contain all the living creatures that I shall spare from destruction. Noe built the ark and entered into it with his family and living creatures of every kind, according to the number designated by the Almighty. The waters of the flood then overflowed the earth and all flesh was destroyed that moved upon it (*Gen.* vi.). Thus did the God of justice punish sinners. What lot have we to expect? Is there no protection for us—no ark of safety? The ark of Noe, says St. Bernard, was the symbol of the ark of grace—of Mary the mother of God. The ark of Noe was a means of preservation from the waters of the deluge; Mary is the means of preservation from shipwreck through sin. Noe built the ark in order to escape the deluge; Christ prepared Mary for himself, that he might redeem the human race. Through the ark, eight persons alone were saved; through Mary, all men are invited to eternal life (*Serm. de S. M.*). St. Bernard was untiring in exhorting sinners to have recourse, with confidence, to Mary, in order to obtain sorrow and forgiveness for their sins. To excite still greater devotion in our hearts to this Holy Mother, let us consider that she is the hope of all, and of sinners in particular.

I.

We are all children of God, but being endowed with free will, we choose, some of us to be dutiful, and others, undutiful children. The ways of the virtuous are different, as well as the ways of the wicked. Among the good, some cultivate particularly one virtue, some another; of the wicked, some devote themselves to riches, others to honors, others to pleasures. Experience teaches us that the wicked outnumber the virtuous. Many are called but few are chosen. The great reason of this is to be found in the frequency and force of temptation! Our enemy aims at nothing less than the total ruin of our souls, and to compass this, he exerts all his malice, spite, power, and vigilance. How difficult it is to resist his suggestions—to discover his deceptions! No man on earth is valiant and wise enough to contend with him successfully. He possesses wisdom, courage, prudence, intelligence, far superior to ours, and all these are made subservient to insatiable malice and zeal for the eternal destruction of man. He never suffers infirmity, because he is immortal; he is never wearied, because he is indefatigable; he is never checked by remorse, because he is incorrigible; he cannot be moved by entreaties, because he is dead to every feeling of pity and mercy. He is at one time a serpent, at another a lion, using violence and fraud, open war, and clandestine surprise. His auxiliaries are the world and the flesh—the world with its pomp and vanities, the flesh with its flattering allurements. He draws opportunity from everything. He makes use of ourselves to destroy us. He corrupts the feelings of the heart, disturbs the humors of the body, throws into confusion the ideas of the mind, and combats us, not only by wickedness, but also by apparent virtue. If we are timid, he overwhelms us insultingly; if we imagine ourselves strong for the fight, he overcomes us without battle; if we sometimes succeed in defeating him, he returns to the contest more impetuously than before. This is a brief sketch of a man's sad life of temptations on earth.

Mary is our hope in this land of sorrow and trial. Mary, with all the fond tenderness of a mother, assists her devout servants to persevere in virtue and live a life of grace and holiness. She is the great woman promised to mankind, who was to repair the evil caused by our first mother, Eve, and crush the head of the deceiving serpent. I will put enmities, saith God to the serpent, between thee and the woman, and thy seed and her seed, she shall crush thy head (*Gen.* iii. 15). The serpent is the devil, the woman is Mary; her seed is Christ, the Divine Word made man in the bosom of Mary. The ruin of the human race and the empire of Satan had beginning from a woman. From the Holy Virgin took rise the reparation of man and the destruction of sin. The enemy, like a serpent concealed in the grass, lies in wait for the children of God; but all his schemes are frustrated through the patronage of Mary. According to St. Bernard, the Blessed Virgin is the famous warrior-woman who first made war against our enemy, who defeated and prostrated him, and still, holding him in slavery beneath her feet, restrains him from destroying the children of God.

Whilst the Israelites, exiled from their own country, were in servitude in the empire of Persia, the fair Esther, amongst many maidens selected for their beauty, found most favor with Assuerus. The king, in a great assembly of all the princes of the empire, placed the royal diadem upon her head, and made her queen instead of Vasthi. Sometime after, the king advanced Aman, and set his throne above all the princes that were with him. And all the king's servants that were at the doors of the palace, bent their knees and worshipped Aman, for so the emperor had commanded them; only Mardochai did not bend his knee, or worship him (*Esth.* iii. 1, 2). Aman was filled with indignation at this want of respect on the part of Mardochai; and calling together his friends, and Zares his wife, declared to them the greatness of his riches and with how great glory the king had advanced him above all his princes and servants. And whereas, he added, I have all these things, I think I have nothing so long as I see Mardochai, the Jew, sitting before the king's gate (*Ibid.* v. 10-12). He then prevailed upon the king to publish an edict, commanding that all the Hebrews in the empire should be killed and destroyed on the same day. When Mardochai had heard these things he rent his garments and put on sackcloth, strewing ashes on his head. And in all provinces, towns, and places, to which the king's cruel edict was come, there was great mourning among the Jews, with fasting, wailing, and weeping. The proud Aman was exultant; but punishment soon followed his crime. Mardochai and the Jews reposed all their hopes in Esther; and she, by her prayers, induced the king to recall the bloody edict. Aman was hung upon the gibbet which he had erected for Mardochai; and to the Jews a new light seemed to arise, joy, honor, and exultation. All the sacred expositors apply this fact to Mary. St. Bonaventure writes: The favor of Mary delivers from eternal death all those whom she wishes to deliver. This was prefigured in queen Esther. The king loved her above all the other women, and placed the diadem upon her head. By power with the king, Esther obtained the crown of royalty and saved her people from extermination. Mary found such favor with the eternal King of ages, that she became queen of heaven and earth, and brought succor to the human race delivered over to death (*Spec. B. V. c.* 5). St. Anselm exclaims, What thanks shall I return to the Mother of God, my Lord, through whose fruitfulness I have been ransomed from slavery and snatched from eternal death ; by whose offspring I have been restored to life, and recalled from an exile of misery to the country of celestial happiness ? The most Holy Virgin, the most perfect among mere creatures, rendered herself so dear to the Lord by her fairness and her virtues, that he selected her for his mother and associated her with himself in the work of redemption. Who will deny to Mary the power to save sinners from the anger of God ? What Christian will hesitate to place his every hope in Mary ?

II.

All have much to hope from the patronage of Mary, but sinners have the most powerful motives for hope. When a father is in anger against an ungrateful son, what does the son do to conciliate anew the love of his father? He hastens to his mother, acknowledges his disobedience, his misconduct, expresses his regret, and his determination to offend no more, declares to her that he dares not approach his father, and entreats her to interpose her influence. The fond mother rejoices to see her wayward son repentant, appeals earnestly to the father, and desists not from her kind efforts until she effects a reconciliation between father and son. By sinning we offer insult to the infinite majesty of a God who is holiness by essence; so that he no longer regards us as his people, no longer as his children. He turns his face away from us in anger. Left to ourselves, we can do nothing meritorious of eternal life. Were death to come upon us in this state, we should be lost forever. But Mary, seeing our disposition to penitence, obtains pardon for us by her urgent entreaties, and restores us to grace and to the rights of the children of heaven.

Is Mary, exclaims St. Bonaventure, the mother of Christ alone? No, assuredly; she is likewise the universal mother of all the faithful. If Christ, says St. Ambrose, is the brother of believers, why is not Mary, who gave him birth, the mother of believers? Let us rejoice, therefore, and cry out with rapture, Blessed is the brother through whom Mary is our mother, and blessed is the mother through whom Christ is our brother. The mother of God is then our mother. The mother of him in whom we trust, and whom alone we have to fear, is also our own mother. Thou, O Mary, subjoins St. Bernard, art mother of the king and the exile; mother of the culprit and the judge; mother of God and of man. Being mother of the one and the other, thou canst not suffer them to remain in discord. If sin condemns the sinner, says St. Bonaventure, the protection of Mary recalls him to life and preserves him living. O, the wonderful mercy of the Lord our God, who, to enable us to avoid the rigor of his justice, not only gave us a mediator in Christ, but a zealous advocate in Mary!

The Lord commanded Moses to place upon the ark the propitiatory, covered with plates of the purest gold. Two cherubim stood at the sides covering the propitiatory with their wings and forming a kind of throne, on which the Lord was believed to sit and receive the prayers and vows of his people, and render thence his answers and his oracles, and make known his will (*Ex.* xxv. 17–22). Mary, writes a devout and learned servant of hers, is the universal propitiatory. Thence God speaks to the heart of men, and gives responses of kindness and pardon; thence he distributes his treasures, and thence all kinds of blessings flow to man. St. Germanus thus invokes Mary: Thou art my encouragement, thou my only guide in my earthly pilgrimage, thou the strength of my weakness, thou the wealth of my poverty, the medicine of my infirmities, the consolation of my sorrows; thou art my liberator from captivity, thou art the hope of my salvation. Hear my prayers; have compassion on my sighs. Thou art my queen, my refuge, my life, my help, my hope, my strength. Mary is, therefore, the hope of all Christians, but especially of sinners. By having recourse to her with confidence, they readily obtain forgiveness from Almighty God.

ASPIRATION.

On the day of judgment deliver us, Holy Virgin Mary.

PRACTICE.

Repeat, with great devotion, the Angelic Salutation.

LITANY.

Read Creator and Creature, by Father Faber.

TWENTY-SIXTH DAY.

MARY OUR GUIDE TO HEAVEN.

"As the Morning Star in the midst of a cloud." *Eccl.* i. 6.

WHEN a man is born into the world, his mother smiles upon him and forgets her sorrows. But the man arrives a stranger, and enters upon a life full of bitterness, toil, and misery. As if anticipating the ills which await him, before he opens his eyes to the light of day, he bathes them with tears; before a smile enlivens his lips, he distorts them with lamentations; before he speaks, he groans and complains. All this only foreshadows the afflictions which man is destined to encounter in life. Holy Job calls the world a land of misery and darkness; and the life of man a warfare on earth. Whether we consider the internal tumults by which man is harassed, or the dangers which on all sides surround him without, we shall find that his life has a perfect image in a tempestuous ocean which threatens a shipwreck at every moment. The monsters of the deep, its frightful whirlpools, its insidious quicksands, the continual agitation of its billows, are appropriate images of the passions of the human heart —their turbulence and inconstancy. The pirates which infest the seas, the tempests which darken the heavens, are vivid images of the dangers which encompass man and threaten him with eternal destruction. If the unfortunate mariner is overtaken by the tempest during the obscurity of night, and by the fury of winds driven out of his course, what recourse is left to him? None, unless his friendly star looks out through the parting clouds, and points out the way to a port of safety. Have we a friendly star in the stormy ocean of life? Our star is Mary, says St. Ambrose (*de B. V.*), and all Christians should turn their eyes to her, and direct the course of their life according to her example. If we do this we shall not be driven about by the breath of vain glory; we shall not be dashed to pieces against the resistance of enemies; we shall not be swallowed up by the whirlpool of pleasures, but shall arrive safely at the harbor of eternal peace. Influenced by these considerations, the Church salutes Mary as Star of the Sea— Hail, Star of the Sea! and Mary is a faithful star and guides to heaven both the just man and the sinner.

I.

St. Thomas teaches (*Op.* 8) that the especial reason why the Blessed Virgin was named Mary, is, that she was enlightened. And, indeed, Mary was so enlightened by the grace of God, that she was able to communicate light to the whole world. As the sun and moon, among the celestial bodies, shed the greatest abundance of light over the face of the earth, Mary is likened to the sun and moon. Mary was enlightened by God, adds St. Bonaventure (*in Spec. C.* 13), and she enlightens the universe with the numerous favors of her mercy and charity. Fair is the moon, says St. Peter Damian, and although it obscures the smaller stars, it does not prevent them from sending down to us some rays of light; but when the sun rises majestically in the east, it diffuses splendor throughout the world; and whilst it brings full day to us, it completely overpowers the brightness of all the stars. In like manner the Blessed Virgin shines resplendent in grace above angels and men (*Serm. de Annunt*). St. Thomas teaches (*Op.* 8) that the

Lord infused a threefold fulness of grace into the Blessed Virgin; the first was a fulness of sufficiency, the second of abundance, and the third of excellency. The first he bestowed upon her the very moment of her sanctification; the second when the incarnation was accomplished; and the third accompanied every action of her life, and rendered her incomparable in the exercise of every virtue.

The grace of Mary was immeasurably greater and more sublime than the grace of angels and saints; because she was not only exalted to be queen of angels and men, but was also destined to be the immaculate mother of the Most High. Besides sanctifying grace, we receive in Baptism and the other sacraments other graces, by which we are enabled to practise good works and merit the eternal possession of God; but the grace conferred upon the Blessed Virgin, in her sanctification, was grace preparing her for the most sublime dignity of Mother of God. The difference between the grace of Mary and that of the other saints is immense; Mary, from her conception, was appointed Mother of God; the other saints were destined to enjoy the vision of God in heaven. If all the graces bestowed upon Mary had for their principal object her dignity of Mother of him who is the light of the world, we may justly conclude that Mary was enlightened in order that she also might furnish light to us.

The miraculous pillar, which the Lord caused to appear to the Israelites in the wilderness, guided them faithfully during all of their wanderings, until they reached the land of promise. As soon as the sun appeared above the horizon it assumed a dusky hue, and became a pillar of a cloud; but when the sun disappeared it became a pillar of fire, and glowing like a new sun, illuminated the encampments of the Israelites. Sacred expositors teach that the pillar of light was, amongst other things, a symbol of the Blessed Virgin. She was never in darkness, says St. Jerome (*in Ps.* lxxvii.), but always in light. O Holy Virgin, exclaims St. Epiphanius (*Orat. de Laud. V.*), thou art a shining star who didst draw down light from heaven—Christ our Lord—to enlighten the minds of mortals. Celestial cloud, irradiated by the Holy Ghost, thou didst bring into the world the Savior of the human race; beneficent cloud, thou didst cause the heavenly dew of the Holy Spirit to fall upon the earth and produce the fruits of faith. O vivifying cloud, cries out St. Andrew of Crete (*Orat. de Deip.*), who guided with thy light not the carnal people of Israel, but Christian nations to the knowledge of the ineffable light of God! The miraculous cloud, therefore, which appeared to the Israelites in the wilderness, signified not only Christ, who came to enlighten the whole world with the light of his grace, but the Blessed Virgin also, who, with Christ, and after Christ enlightens the universe. That pillar of light enabled the Israelites to avoid the perils of the night; the light with which Mary favors her servants enables them to avoid the dangers of sin and perdition. That cloud conducted the children of Israel safely to the land of Chanaan; Mary guides us through this wicked and treacherous world and finally leads us to eternal happiness.

God in his wisdom and goodness wished us to possess in his Son an advocate with himself, and in Mary an advocate with his Son. Our ruin commenced with a woman, and with a woman likewise the Lord wished our reparation to begin. By one woman, says St. Augustine (*Serm. 13 de Nat.*), death entered into the world, and by one woman, also, the Holy Virgin, life and salvation were restored to man. By means of Eve the light of original grace was extinguished, and by means of Mary it was rekindled in the world. Her Son Jesus is the triumphant light of grace which alone can conduct to heaven.

II.

Christ our Savior, wishing to impress us with the greatness of his solicitude for our welfare, assumes the character of a shepherd. I am the Good Shepherd (*John* x. 14), the shepherd of your souls, and I feed them in the pastures of divine grace, that you may possess eternal life. As such he is represented in the Spouse of the Canticles. But who is mystically shadowed forth in his spouse? All interpreters with one voice reply that, under the name of spouse, is signified the Church, the just soul, and the Virgin Mary. Mary, therefore, has the character of a divine shepherdess. The good shepherd feeds his flock, conducts it on the way, and protects it. Mary, then, as our shepherdess by divine appointment, must perform for us the same kind offices. She feeds us with the example of her virtues. Let the virginity and life of Mary, writes St. Ambrose, be ever

present to your minds; in her as in a
mirror, the image of chastity and of every
virtue is reflected. Study the examples of
her life, there you will discover what is to
be amended, what is to be shunned, and
what is to be practised (*Lib.2 de B. M.*).
Imitate, exhorts St. Ildephonsus, the Blessed Virgin and the saints, whom you glorify; our commendation is not so advantageous to them as their imitation is to us.
The divine spouse is much better pleased
with a devout imitator than with an idle
eulogizer. True, heartfelt praise, however, consists in imitating the deeds of the
person praised (*Serm. de Assumpt.*).
Mary, therefore, proposes to sinners the
imitation of her virtues; firm faith, immovable hope, untiring charity, profound
humility.

The sinner, being blinded in the understanding, has need of a guide to conduct
him on the way. But where shall we
find a better guide than Mary? As the
Lord made his star appear to the wise
men of the east to lead them to the cra-
dle of the Savior of the world, so he has
given to sinners a mystic star, Mary, to be
their guide to the kingdom of heaven.
When the flock wanders off into rough
and dangerous places, what does the good
shepherd? He hastens after them, turns

them back, and directs them to grassy plains and smooth, sloping hills. When Mary sees a Christian dangerously urged to sin by violent temptation or vicious inclinations, she speeds to his side and entices him back to the path of virtue. Mary, according to St. Bernard (*Serm.* 4 *de Nat. V.*),dispenses the life of divine wisdom and the dew of celestial grace. If a wild beast assails the flock, the shepherd immediately stands forth in its defense. But who shall defend us in the midst of so many enemies? We shall fall a prey to their fury, unless we place ourselves under the protection of the divine shepherdess, Mary. Our perfidious enemy seeks to destroy us by deceptions and temptations; but we have nothing to fear if Mary combats in our behalf. Her power is extremely great, and according to the saints, at the sole mention of her name every creature reverently bends the knee, and the infernal spirits are scattered like a cloud in presence of the sun.

ASPIRATION.

Hail, Star of the Sea, Mother of God, and Gate of Heaven.

PRACTICE.

Entreat the Blessed Virgin to obtain for you grace to grow in the love of God every day.

LITANY.

Read Father Burke's Sermon on "Mary, Star of the Sea."

TWENTY-SEVENTH DAY.

MARY, HEALTH OF THE WEAK.

''Moses made a brazen serpent and set it up for a sign.'' *Num.* xxi. 9.

THE Hebrews were marching through the vast wilderness of Arabia, and turning to the right or to the left, according to the movements of the miraculous cloud given to them by the Almighty for a guide. The Lord, like a loving Father, provided for their wants, supplying them with water and healthy food in the midst of the barrenness of the arid desert. After having marched to Mount Hor, on the confines of Edom, the people began to be weary of their journey and labor; and, speaking against God and Moses they said, Why didst thou bring us out of Egypt to die in the wilderness ? Why have you brought us into this wretched place, which cannot be sowed, nor bringeth forth figs nor vines nor pomegranates, neither is there any water to drink? There is no bread, and our soul loatheth this very light food. Wherefore the Lord sent among the people fiery serpents, which bit them and killed many of them. The people repented, and acknowledged their sin, and Moses prayed for the people ; and the Lord said to him, Make a brazen serpent, and set it up for a sign; whoever, being struck, shall look upon it, shall live (*Num.* **xx.** 19). Christ himself instructs us to recognize in this miraculous serpent the virtue of his cross; on it he was to be lifted up for the salvation of all those who were perishing from the bite of the serpent of destruction. But is not the Most Holy Virgin also signified in the serpent of the desert? It was given to the Hebrews, that by looking on it those who were bitten might obtain life and health. Mary has been given to Christians, that in their infirmities, whether spiritual or corporal, they might find relief and health in her protection. Hence the Church, in her liturgy, honors the Blessed Virgin with the glorious title of Health of the Weak.

I.

God in the beginning created man immortal, and constituted him in sanctifying grace. After a certain time of probation on earth, he was to have mounted to heaven in body and soul, there to enter into the possession of eternal bliss. Adam, by transgressing the command of God, forfeited sanctity and justice, and incurred the anger. of the Lord and the penalty of death. Man by sin was thus reduced, both in soul and body, to a condition far different from that in which he had been constituted. Sin is, therefore, the source of all the evils which afflict us. To the soul, it is the cause of the loss of grace and original innocence; and to the body, it is the cause of death and all the evils which pervade it. As soon as Adam sinned, death began to germinate in his being, and, in virtue of the eternal decrees it is to germinate in all his posterity. In his early years man grows like a flower of spring; the rose of health tinges his cheeks, and robustness nerves his frame; still in his whole body, in his very veins and sinews, the agents of death are quietly at work and decay and dissolution are the inevitable result. We are dying every day. And do we not perceive that our strength is daily wearing away? The variableness of the seasons, heat and cold and the unhealthfulness of the atmosphere, hunger, thirst, exposure, accidents, diseases, are engaged in the service of death every hour and render our life one of weakness and sorrow.

Our comfort in life is our tender mother Mary. She, by the power which she enjoys from God, can heal all our infirmities. God in his goodness has given to us human means of health, and these we are to employ; but our sovereign remedy is Mary. She gave birth to the Physician, she produced the Medicine of the human race (*St. Bernardin. Serm. de B. V.*). Whilst our divine Redeemer was preaching his heavenly doctrine, he confirmed his teachings by miracles, and there was no land or city through which he passed that could not boast of many cures performed by him. In this, according to the Fathers, Jesus Christ had two principal objects in view: the one to give relief to languishing humanity, he being the father of men ; the other, that the witnesses of these prodigies might believe in him and embrace the faith which he announced. In this way, whilst he restored soundness to the body, he bestowed health upon the soul. Mary acts in a similar manner with us, she obtains health for the infirm in order to draw them more easily to God. Temporal favors are always granted with a view to the spiritual life. We do not read of Mary, that she gave health to any one whilst she remained on earth ; but now that she is reigning in heaven, she is most prodigal in bestowing such blessings on those who devoutly invoke her. There is no kind of infirmity, or misfortune, or tribulation, which Mary possesses not the power to heal. To this bear witness the countless votive tablets which are suspended around her altars in all the cities of every Christian land. · How many have been raised by Mary from sickness to health! To how many has speech and hearing and sight been restored through her intercession! How many have escaped all the horrors of shipwreck through the interposition of her power!

The Blessed Virgin banishes famine,

and feeds the starving. She acts toward us like the widow of Sarephta, who gave bread to Elias languishing with hunger. Mary quenches thirst. She was prefigured, according to commentators, in the fair Rebecca who, being asked for a draught of water by the servant of Abraham, gave drink not only to him but also to his camels. Mary, as the spouse of the Canticles, is the fountain of gardens, the well of living waters(*Cant.* iv. 15). St. Methodius teaches that Mary was prefigured in the cistern of Bethlehem, so ardently desired by David, to refresh him in his burning thirst(*Orat. in Hypap.*). St. Epiphanius salutes Mary in the following words: Hail, full of grace, thou who dost refresh the thirsty with the sweetness of perennial waters. Mary is, therefore, the health of the weak and the comfort of the afflicted. In our infirmities we have reason to hope more from her kindness than from physical and temporal remedies.

II.

The soul is liable to infirmities as well as the body; and, as the soul is a far more noble substance than the body, its infirmities are more pernicious. The infirmities of the body hasten temporal death; but those of the soul lead to death eternal. The infirmities of the soul are evil passions. Our fever, says St. Ambrose, is avarice, impurity, anger, ambition. Infirmities of the soul are, also, the darkness and ignorance of the understanding, the tendency to evil of the will, the violence of concupiscence, the assaults of the world, the devil, and the flesh, fears, suspicions, weariness, and discontent of mind and heart.

By the sins of our first parents, we were injured not only in body, but also, and particularly, in the faculties of the soul; and hence it is that we so frequently abandon ourselves to our corrupt inclinations and become guilty of sin. But the Blessed Virgin, by her powerful patronage, defends us against evil, and heals all our infirmities, if we invoke her protection with devotion and confidence. We need light to dissipate the darkness of our understanding. This light is procured for us by Mary. She obtains knowledge for the ignorant and instruction for the untutored. She was prefigured in the wise Debbora, who, seated under a palm tree, instructed the ch'ldren of Israel in their duties; and also in the prophetess Holda, who explained to the ignorant people the things of God. Mary strengthens the will to seek with constancy what is praiseworthy. She gives salutary counsel for the rejection of evil and the performance of good; she excites contempt of the world in the heart of man, and infuses the love of virtue; she disengages the affections from transitory and earthly things, and transfers them to God alone; she furnishes man with courage to shake off the infamous yoke of the devil, to overcome the enticements of the flesh, to restrain the fury of concupiscence, to break the chains of sinful habits ; she disposes him for the desire of eternal blessings, and leads him to operate justice and righteousness. Hence she is compared to the serpent raised by Moses in the wilderness, by lifting their eyes to which, those who had been bitten by venomous serpents recovered their wonted health. She is compared to the pond of Jerusalem, called Probatica, which had the virtue of making whole of whatsoever infirmity he lay under, him that went down first into the pond after the motion of the water (*John* v. 4).

All that has been said of Mary is confirmed by the Fathers and saints of the Church. Mary, writes one of her devout servants, is the refuge of sinners, the secure asylum of those who are suffering under temptation or calamity or persecution. She is the most liberal dispenser of favors and the merciful mother of all the faithful. Mary, writes St. Andrew of Crete, is the propitiatory of the whole world. Through her the Lord speaks to the heart and bestows pardon; through her he shows himself appeased, forgives crimes, and distributes his divine blessings; from her every good derives to us, for she is assiduous in her supplications for the unfortunate. St. John of Damascus, apostrophizing the Blessed Virgin, exclaims: Having trust in thee I shall be saved; with thy protection I shall have nothing to fear; with thy patronage, thy assistance as a breastplate, I shall attack my enemies and put them to flight (*Orat. de Annunt.*). Mary, therefore, is the health of the weak in weakness, both of soul and body.

ASPIRATION.

Teach me to rule my tongue, Most Blessed Virgin Mary.

PRACTICE.

Perform some act or recite some prayer in honor of Mary, morning, noon, and night.

LITANY.

Read Our Lady of Lourdes.

TWENTY-EIGHTH DAY.

MARY, PROTECTRESS OF CHRISTIANS.

"If I have found favor in thy sight, O King, and if it please thee, give me my life for which I ask, and my people for which I request." *Es_ther* vii. 3.

KING ASSUERUS had already signed the fatal edict against the Jews, and the perfidious Aman had commanded the governors of all the provinces of the empire to exterminate all the Hebrews under their authority. The edict struck the Jews with consternation. They clothed themselves with sackcloth, and sprinkled ashes upon their heads, and filled the air with cries and lamentations. Mardochai entreated Esther to interpose in behalf of her people, and obtain the revocation of the edict. She presented herself before Assuerus, and pleased his eyes; and he said to her: What is thy petition, Esther, that it may be granted to thee? and what wilt thou have done? Although thou ask the half of my kingdom, thou shalt have it. Then she answered: If I have found favor in thy sight, O king, and if it please thee, give me my life for which I ask, and my people for which I request (*Esth.* vii. 2, 3). The anger of Assuerus was appeased; the edict was revoked; and a new light of joy and honor rose to the Jews (viii. 16). Who is ignorant that Mary was prefigured in the heroines of the Old Testament? That the Fathers recognize in Esther protecting the Hebrews, a figure of Mary, the protectress of the Christians? Aman had vowed the destruction of Israel, but Assuerus, yielding to the prayers of Esther, pardoned the Jews, and took them into favor. Satan has resolved upon the ruin of all Christians and wages incessant war against them; but shielded by the protection of Mary, who shall be able to overcome us?   And Mary displays especial kindness in protecting Christians against their enemies.

I.

The holy Scriptures teach us that God has assigned an angel guardian to man. The Psalmist says: He hath given his angels charge over thee, to keep thee in all thy ways. In their hands they shall bear thee up; lest thou dash thy foot against a stone. Thou shalt walk upon the asp and the basilisk; and thou shalt trample under foot the lion and the dragon (*Ps.* xc. 10). We 'learn from the prophet Daniel that the kingdom of the Persians and that of the Greeks were placed under the guardianship of angels ; and it is the common opinion of the Fathers, that besides kingdoms, dioceses also, cities and their communities, each have their guardian angel. But to whom has the Lord intrusted the guardianship of the whole Christian family ? To the Blessed Virgin, the help of Christians, who is as the defending angel of all the faithful. But at what time was granted to us this angel of defence ? The Savior was hanging upon the cross, the work of redemption was about to be consummated. Around the cross stood Mary and John, Mary of Cleophas and Mary Magdalen. The Savior bends down his dying eyes and beholds his mother and his beloved disciple. He wishes to give a last proof of love to St· John, and in him to all who should believe in himself; and he says to his mother· Behold thy son; and to his disciple: Behold thy mother; and from that hour the disciple took her to his own (*John* xix. 26). Jesus thus provided for Mary a filial companion, and for all the faithful a most loving mother. After the death of the Savior she was regarded by the apostles and all believers as a mother. She strengthened the weak, consoled the afflicted, assured the doubtful, and confirmed them all in the faith of the resurrection (*Corn. a Lap. in Joan,* C. 19). After this life Mary passed to heaven, and there reigning in glory she watches over and protects her servants. But the Holy Virgin was our mother before the tragedy of Calvary. Being Mother of the Head, writes William of Paris (*in Cant.* 4), she became mother of the members. Mary is the mother of Christ, therefore of the members of Christ. Christ is our head ; by giving birth bodily to the Head, Mary gave birth spiritually to the members. Hence she is called mother by all Christians, and by all is honored as a mother should be honored. Richard of St. Lawrence (*C.* 2 *de B. V.*) styles her mother of Christ by nature and beneficent mother of Christians by grace. And Mary has indeed the heart of a mother, for she is watching over us continually to aid us, succor us, and save us from perishing.

It has been already observed that Mary is the angel given by the Almighty to all Christians, as a body, to keep them in all their ways. We read in Genesis (xlviii. 16) that God gave to Jacob an angel that delivered him from all evils. It is the office therefore of angels to deliver men from the evils and dangers that threaten them. Mary discharges this office most faithfully in our regard. The world is full of perils. They are met with, according to St. Paul, in journeys, in rivers, in false brothers, in cities, in solitudes, in labor, in affliction, in hunger, thirst, and nakedness. St. John admonishes us, that all that is in the world is the concupiscence of the flesh, and the concupiscence of the eyes, and the pride of life (1 *John* ii. 16). But Mary, after God, is our deliverer. Whilst living, says St. Bonaventure (*Spec.C.* 8), she had compassion on the unfortunate ; but far greater is her mercy now, and far more abundant the graces which she obtains for us. We read in the book of Tobias (viii. 3), that the angel Raphael, who served as guide for Tobias, took the devil and bound him in the desert of Upper Egypt. It is a part, therefore, of the office of the angels to resist the devil and prevent him from doing injury. The prince of apostles teaches us (1 *Pet.* v. 8) that our adversary, the devil, as a roaring lion, goeth about, seeking whom he may devour. But the Almighty has bestowed upon Mary so great power over the temptation of the devil, that as soon as one of her devout servants, attacked by him, implores her assistance, at one sign of her presence he takes to flight covered with confusion (*St. Brig. Rev.*). We find in Exodus that the Lord said to his people through Moses: Behold 1 will send my angel, who shall go before thee, and keep thee in thy journey, and bring thee into the place that I have prepared. Take notice of him, and hear his voice, and do not think him one to be contemned; for he will not forgive when thou hast sinned, and my name is in him. But if thou wilt hear his voice, and do all that I speak, I will be an enemy to thy enemies, and will afflict them that afflict thee (xxiii.

20). Is not Mary the angel sent us by Almighty God to suggest good thoughts to our mind that we may embrace good and avoid evil? If he commanded Moses and the Israelites to honor their angel, will he not require as much of all Christians? Will he not insist upon their tributing due honor to his own, and our Most Holy Mother? Let us address Mary, with St. Bonaventure (*in Spec. c.* 6): O great Lady, by that power which was conferred upon thee, in view of thy sublime dignity of Mother of God, thou hast sway over the demons; restrain therefore their audacity that they may not work us harm; as Queen of angels, keep our welfare in view and command the angels subject to thy authority to defend us against the temptations of the infernal spirits. ·

It is registered in the book of the Apocalypse, that it belongs to the angels to offer up our prayers before the throne of God. And another angel came and stood before the altar, having a golden censer ; and there was given him much incense, that he should offer the prayers of all saints upon the golden altar which is before the throne of God. And the smoke of the incense of the prayers of the saints ascended up before God from the hand of the angel (viii. 3, 4). It is certain that every grace flows from God, and that every best gift is from above, coming down from the Father of lights, with whom there is no change nor shadow of vicissitude (*James* 1. 17).   But as Christ intercedes for us with the Father, we are favored with the intercession of the angels, the apostles, the patriarchs, the prophets, the martyrs, the confessors and the virgins; but far greater excellence, far greater virtue, does the intercession of the ever blessed Virgin possess.   What they united can accomplish, says St. Anselm, she alone can more easily perform; for she is the queen of the angels and of all the saints.   Mary in a certain manner merited to be the mother of the Redeemer and the Judge of mankind.   Who could be more powerful, therefore, to draw down the favors of the Redeemer and appease the anger of the Judge?

When Esther presented herself before Assuerus, she said: If I have found favor in thy sight, O king, and if it please thee, give my life for which I ask, and my people for which I request.   For we are given up, I and my people, to be destroyed, to be slain, and to perish. Esther had before requested Mardochai to gather together all the Jews in Susan, and pray to the Lord for her. In presenting herself before Assuerus she united the prayers of the people with her own, and the anger of the king was appeased. Mary acts in a similar manner in our behalf. If Assuerus yielded to the prayers of Esther, will not the Almighty be propitiated by the prayers of Mary? Richard of St. Lawrence, speaking of the prayers of Mary says, She not only can entreat her Son, like the other saints, to have compassion on her servants, but she can employ with her Son her authority as his mother. When the angel declared to her that the Lord was with her, he indicated her dignity and her authority with her Son. Whilst of the other saints it is said that they are with the Lord, of Mary it is said that the Lord is with her. Mary is the Protectress of Christians.

ASPIRATION.

From anger and hatred and all perverseness of will, deliver me, Holy Virgin Mary.

PRACTICE.

Thank Mary frequently for the favors which she has obtained for you.

LITANY.

Read the Book of Esther.

TWENTY-NINTH DAY.

MARY, CONSOLER OF THE AFFLICTED.

"Among the cities which you shall give to the Levites, six shall be separated for refuge to fugitives." *Num.* xxxv. 6.

THE goodness and justice of God are both infinite. He rewards the just in proportion to their merits, and punishes the wicked according to their misdeeds. With this principle in view, he issued the commandments on Mount Sinai. He also prescribed that the guilty should be subjected to temporal punishment, even to the punishment of death. But in his mercy he set apart six cities amongst those assigned to the tribes of Levi, to serve as places of refuge for those who should shed blood against their will. Three of these cities were beyond the

Jordan, and three in the land of Chanaan. As the Hebrews in the old law had places of refuge, we, also, in the new law of grace, possess a refuge, and one of peculiar excellence. The asylums of the Hebrews protected those alone who were guilty of involuntary homicide. Our refuge furnishes shelter to all the guilty, even to those stained with the greatest crimes. What city of refuge has been given to us? St. John of Damascus replies that our city of refuge is Mary (*Serm. II. de Dom. V.*). St. Bernard answers, also: In every temptation, in every tribulation, in every necessity, the city of refuge is open to admit us, the bosom of the loving mother (*Serm.* ix. *in. Ps. Qui habit.*). Mary is the holy city seen by St. John. She is the city of refuge, because she reconciles the sinner with God and conducts him to eternal happiness.

I.

Sin is defined by St. Augustine as something said or done or desired in opposition to the eternal law of God; by St. Ambrose, as a breaking of the law of God, and disobedience to the commandments of heaven. It is wrong done the majesty of God by a creature. It is the sovereign evil of all evils; and no effort of the human mind, aided by whatever of deformity and horror the imagination can represent, will ever be able to form a conception of its monstrousness. Sin, says St. Thomas (xix *q.* 71, *a.* 6), is a turning away from God to turn to the creature. This, assuredly, is a great wrong perpetrated against God, and a greater insult could not be offered him. Sin is opposed to the unity of God, giving to the creature a portion of the homage due to God alone. It is opposed to the goodness of God, because, instead of regarding him as the chief good and the source of all that is good, it practically acknowledges in the creature perfection not derived from him. It is opposed to the Incarnation, because it diminishes the benefits produced by it. But what language could express the evil which it brings upon the soul? It withdraws us from God, and binds us to creatures, which are nothing but vanity. It despoils us of grace and virtue, excludes us from eternal bliss, spreads darkness over the understanding, and creates perplexity in the will, torments and tears the conscience, and leads to eternal damnation. Sin is so destructive in its own nature that in this world it causes spiritual death to the soul by depriving it of sanctifying grace—the principle of supernatural life; and in the world to come it causes true death to the soul by depriving it of God. Should we die in mortal sin we are lost forever. If we sin grievously, even once more, may we not be called to our last account without a moment's warning?

Sin impresses a stain upon the soul, and this stain continues until it is washed out by penance and sanctifying grace. Stains, properly speaking, belong to material substances which lose their brightness by coming in contact with another body; but they are said figuratively to affect the spiritual substance of the soul. The soul possesses twofold purity: the one is derived from the natural light of reason, by which the soul is guided in its natural operations; the other, from the light of grace, by which man is fitted for supernatural works. When the soul attaches itself to some object, it comes, as it were, in contact with it. But by sinning the soul attaches itself to what is contrary to the light of reason and the law of God; hence, the prejudice to purity which arises from such a contact is metaphorically called a stain of the soul. This stain is not any thing positive in the soul, nor does it signify privation simply, but a privation of purity or brightness in the soul with reference to sin which is its cause; and as sins admit many varieties, so the stains of the soul which arise from them are various. When the soul, therefore, endowed by the Almighty with the light of reason, and enriched with the light of grace, wilfully extinguishes by sin the light of grace and receives the stamp of iniquity, it must necessarily be regarded with abhorrence by the Author of reason and grace.

When a man has committed a grievous offence against the sovereign authority, and knows that, sooner or later, the matter will be investigated and the merited punishment decreed, what does the conscience-stricken offender? He repents of his deed; he is tortured by fear; he finds no peace amongst his friends; he withdraws from society; he flies for refuge to some distant or solitary place. His only hope is that some powerful influence may be brought to bear in his favor and the remission of his punishment be thus obtained. So it is with the sinner. His conscience keeps the memory of his crimes vivid in his mind, and forebodes' the approaching penalty. He becomes inconsolably miserable. Honors, treasures, possessions, amusements, friends, afford

him no consolation. He flies from place
to place, from scene to scene, but he
cannot escape his torment. Even night
brings him little relief, for his very sleep
is restless. He can say with David, I
walked sorrowful all the day long, and
my sin is always against me
(*Ps.* **xxx**vii. 7; l. 5).   But happy are we
to have a mother to watch over us who
not only endeavors to save us from misfortune, but is willing and able to give us
relief after we have brought misfortune
on ourselves. This mother is Mary. The
Church calls her Refuge of Sinners, the
Consoler of the Afflicted. Mary is queen
of heaven and earth. She is the Mother
of God—the Creator of the heavens and
the earth. She shares the dominion and
power of her Son. The flesh of Christ is
the flesh of Mary. If Christ is glorious
as the only-begotten of the Most High
and the Redeemer of man, Mary is glorious as his mother, and his mother by
her own free consent. Hesitate not,
O Mary, says a devout servant of hers, to
take possession of the goods of thy Son.
Proceed with confidence as a queen, as
the mother and spouse of the King of
kings. Sovereignty is, also, by will of
heaven, an undeniable right of thine.
Mary, writes St. Bernard (*in Sign. Mag.*),

is made all things to all; she owes boundless charity to the wise and to the ignorant. She throws open the treasure of her mercy that all may receive from it; the captive, ransom; the weak, health; the afflicted, consolation; the sinner, pardon; and God himself, glory. Justly, therefore, is she invoked as the Consoler of the afflicted.

II.

It cannot be denied that a great tribulation overhangs the sinner at the hour of death, and the more terrible because it is accompanied by the danger of eternal ruin. At that last moment the enemy represents to the sinner all the evil doings of his life. He recalls to his memory his neglect of grace. He portrays to him most vividly the severity of judgment and the rigorous account which he will have to render. He endeavors to frighten him with the thought of time wasted, of the mercy of God abused, of all the horrors of hell deserved by his sins. He omits no effort, no artifice, to create a want of confidence in God's goodness, and to drag the sinner into the abyss of despair. Woe to the sinner, because the devil is come down unto him, having great wrath, knowing that he hath but a short time (*Apoc.* xii. 12).

But the greater the danger of the child, the greater the solicitude of the fond mother. So it is with Mary towards her devout servants in the trials and temptations of death. St. Jerome writes (*Ep.* ii. *ad Eustoch.*). Not only does the Blessed Virgin not neglect to give succor to her dying children, but she herself, in person, aids them in their last struggles, and defends them and protects them against the assaults of our common enemy. God has granted to the Holy Virgin such power over the malignant spirits that they flee at the slightest indication of her will. St. Bonaventure frequently addressed the following prayer to the Blessed Virgin: Holy Mother, in virtue of thy most exalted dignity of the mother of God, thou hast power to rule the demons. Curb their audacity so that they may not do us injury in our last moments, and cause the angels of heaven to descend and guard us.

ASPIRATION.

Holy Mary, obtain for me grace to love Jesus.

PRACTICE.

Give alms in honor of Mary.

LITANY.

Read the Book of the Apocalypse.

THIRTIETH DAY.

DEVOTION TO THE SACRED HEART OF MARY.

"I was exalted as a rose plant in Jericho."
Eccl. xxiv. 18.

GOD is charity; and he that abideth in charity abideth in God, and God in him (1 *John* iv. 16). The annals of our religion furnish us with innumerable examples of true charity. But as in dignity so in charity, Mary is far exalted above all the other saints. She was chosen from eternity to be the mother of God. In time God was united with her, not only by enlightening her and adorning her with grace, but also with a kind of real identity, taking from her his own flesh and blood. Mary corresponded faithfully with the grace bestowed upon her, loving God more ardently than any other saint. She loved God with her whole heart, her whole will, and her whole mind; and with power of heart, will, and mind, assisted by the fulness of grace. For this reason she is compared to a rose plant in Jericho. Besides, according to Albertus Magnus, where there is greater purity there is greater charity; hence the virgin, as purest of all creatures, acknowledges among them no equal in charity. Let us now consider the motives of the devotion to the Sacred Heart of Mary, and learn in what manner we should honor her.

I.

The reasons which induced the Church to approve of the devotion to the Sacred Heart of Jesus were the same which caused the approbation of the devotion to the Sacred Heart of Mary. As the heart is commonly considered the symbol of love and the seat of affections, it was judged proper to pay public honor to the Sacred Heart of Mary, that the minds of the faithful might be thus led to reflect on the

exceeding great love for God and for us
with which Mary was inflamed. The
Church proposed to us the practice of
devotion to the Sacred Heart of Mary to
excite our piety, and increase our love
and gratitude towards Mary the mother
of Jesus. As Mary was most intimately
united with Jesus both in the order of
grace and the order of nature, it is but
reasonable and natural that they who
practise devotion to the Heart of Jesus
should practise it also to the Heart of
Mary. This is indicated in the order of
Providence regarding Mary, and the practice of the Church in honoring her. In
the Incarnation of the word, the substance of Mary became the substance of
her son Jesus. During the private life
of our Savior, Mary was his inseparable
companion. We find them together in
the stable, and in the temple on the day
of the purification. They fled together
into Egypt and returned again. They
dwelt in the same house, sat at the same
table, and on solemn occasions went together to Jerusalem. Mary was with Jesus at the marriage in Cana of Galilee
and at Capharnaum; and tradition in-
forms us that she followed Jesus during
the whole course of his public life. When
she heard of his capture in the garden

she hastened to meet him, and shared in her heart all his sufferings.   She was present when her Son consummated his holocaust of expiation for the redemption of mankind.   Mary, therefore, during the thirty-three years of Christ's life on earth was always with him.

The Church, guided by the Holy Spirit, attributes to Mary, by a kind of appropriation, those titles which in strict propriety belong only to her son—God made man. Christ is our King, Mary our Queen; Christ is our Father, Mary our Mother; Christ is our advocate and mediator, Mary our advocate and mediatrix.   Christ is our hope, the health of the weak, the refuge of sinners, the consoler of the afflicted, and the help of Christians; and the Church in all her liturgy assigns all these titles to Mary.   Christ is for the faithful the mirror of justice, the seat of wisdom and the cause of spiritual joy; and the same, on the authority of the Church, is also Mary.   During our pilgrimage on earth, Christ is our guide and our light, and Mary is the star that directs our steps and conducts us to heaven.   Jesus is King and Lord of patriarchs, prophets, apostles, martyrs, confessors, and virgins; and Mary is celebrated as queen of angels and all the saints.

That Mary was the most highly privileged of all mere creatures cannot be called in question, for she alone was elevated to the most sublime dignity of Mother of God; but she also, of all pure creatures, loved God most ardently. The language of the Fathers of the Church fully justifies this assertion. According to them, Mary was all inflamed with the ardor of charity; and the bush that burned without being consumed was a symbol of her love. Mary loved God in strictness of truth, with her whole heart, her whole soul, and her whole strength. The love which she bore her son was unlimited. The measure of the graces which she received from God was the measure of her love. Her love for God surpassed the love of all creatures; her soul was melted in the intensity of her love. No mind, says St. Jerome (*Serm. de Assumpt.*), no heart, no human power, can conceive or express the greatness of the love of Mary. When the Virgin conceived, writes William the Abbot (*in Cant. c.* 2), she received into her heart as great ardor of love, by virtue of the Holy Spirit, as a mere creature was capable of receiving. Shall we not pay devotion to the Sacred Heart of Mary, the symbol of her love for God?

Mary cherished also a most fervent love for man. Considering the countless evils with which man was afflicted on account of the sin of Adam, she most ardently desired the coming of the promised Messias, the Savior of the world; and she offered continual entreaties to the Father that he would hasten the coming down of the desire of the eternal hills and the expectation of the nations. When she gave her consent to the Incarnation of the Word in her bosom, it was for our spiritual welfare; hence she is deservedly called the Mother of Fair Love, because in the union with Jesus she is our mediatrix and co-operated in our redemption. But it was on Golgotha that Mary displayed the greatness of her love for mankind. It was there, says St. Bernardine, that she saw squandered the price of the world's redemption; the fortitude of the saints in agony; the beautiful above the sons of men covered with blood; the Lord of the Universe hanging between two thieves; the King of heaven treated with insult, and the Author of life yielding up his spirit in death. But the holy Virgin, out of love for us, submitted with unmurmuring resignation. The wills of Jesus and Mary were perfectly united; they both offered one and the same holocaust; Mary in her heart, Jesus by shedding his blood; thus she, in union with Jesus, obtained the salvation of mankind. How great must have been her love for us? And should we not be devout to her Sacred Heart, the symbol of this love?

II.

Having considered the principal motives which should incite us to devotion to the Sacred Heart of Mary, the inquiry remains, In what manner ought we to honor Mary by this devotion? In the same manner which she observed in the exercise of her love for God. Mary loved God with the utmost ardor, and her purity was the measure of her love. We should therefore honor Mary by the especial practice of the two virtues of purity and charity. God possessed Mary in the beginning of his ways, before he gave existence to creatures. When the time of her conception arrived, grace anticipated nature, and she was conceived without stain of sin. In the opinion of the Fathers, Mary enjoyed immediately the use of reason, and was aware of the privilege of grace bestowed upon her. The heart of Mary was deeply impressed with gratitude; and eager to offer to God what she had received from God, at the age of three she consecrated to him in the temple her virginity, by perpetual vow. By this sacrifice she concealed herself from the eyes of the world in order to live to God alone; she withdrew from her parents to be more closely united with her Creator; she made a vow of virginity when the hope of giving birth to the Messias rendered it a reproach to Hebrew women to be childless. After having passed her early years in the exercise of every virtue, she was visited by an angel, and declared the future mother of God.. Mindful of the vow, she inquired how such an event could be accomplished since she had dedicated to the Almighty her virginity? Nor did she yield her consent until assured that no prejudice should happen to her virginity.

If the thought of the favors received from God moved the virgin to offer him her purity, it is clear what feelings were in her heart—how intense was her charity. Mary surpassed all the heroines of the Old Testament. Sara was praised for fidelity; but greater praise was given to Mary, when it was said to her: Blessed art thou who hast believed. Rebecca was renowned as beautiful, but

Mary is called more beautiful than the sun. Rachel was amiable and gained the heart of Jacob; but Mary gained the heart of him whose love wrought a reconciliation between God and man. Lia was fruitful, but far more fruitful Mary; for although she gave birth to one son only, she brought forth many children to salvation. Debbora was extolled for her wisdom; but the virgin was the habitation of wisdom itself. Esther was humble, but far more humble Mary; for God regarded the humility of his handmaid. Judith was valiant, and slew Holofernes; but the valiant Mary crushed the head of the arrogant serpent. Mary's constant practice of virtue proves how greatly she loved the Almighty God. We may therefore conclude with St. Thomas of Villanova (*Conc.* 4. *in Nat. Virg.*), that the virgin by her ardent charity so captivated the heart of Almighty God that he came down into her bosom and took upon himself the nature of man.

ASPIRATION.

Heart of Jesus, grant me heavenly love!
Heart of Mary, obtain for me charity!

PRACTICE.

Every Saturday offer some act of mor-
tification, and practise some devotion, in
honor of the Sacred Heart of Mary.

LITANY.

Read Imitation of the Blessed Virgin.

THIRTY-FIRST DAY.

PERSEVERANCE IN THE LOVE OF MARY.

"He that shall persevere unto the end, he shall
be saved." *Matt.* x. 22.

GOD in his goodness and wisdom, created men for eternal happiness in
heaven.　As God, in the doctrine of St.
Thomas, grants graces corresponding
to the end and dignity to which he destines men in this life, there can be no
doubt that he bestows upon every man
the graces necessary for the gaining of
heaven, his last end.　When the soul
is united with the body it is stained with

original sin; but man is purified of this stain in baptism, and sanctifying grace is infused into him, and the germ of the holy virtues by the exercise of which he can work out his eternal salvation. But to be actually saved, man must persevere in living virtuously to the last moment of his existence. He that shall persevere to the end shall be saved.

Applying now to the Blessed Virgin what has been said respecting God, he who wishes to have Mary for an advocate must persevere in devotion to her. Not without a hidden meaning is she compared with the cedar, the cypress, and the olive; and it is that, whilst she is unfailing in protecting us and obtaining for us grace from God, we should exert ourselves to persevere in her love and devotion. He who loves God must love his holy Mother. Love for God cannot exist without love for the saints. To close the pious exercise of the month of May, let us gather together the chief motives which urge us to honor Mary with perseverance and consider briefly in what manner our love for her should manifest itself in our actions; always bearing in mind that he that shall persevere unto the end, he shall be saved.

I.

The first motive which should incite us to love and honor Mary perseveringly, is the peculiar love which the Almighty bears her as the fairest among all creatures. To love God means nothing less than to do his holy will; we, therefore, if we wish to love God, should love Mary above all the saints, because above all the saints is she loved by the Almighty. This spouse of the heavenly Solomon came out of the mouth of the Most High, the first-born before all creatures (*Eccl.* xxiv. 5). Many others were dear to God, but she was beloved above them all. There are young maidens without number. One is my dove; my perfect one is but one (*Cant.* vi. 7, 8). God loved the heroines of the old law, but more than all of them he loved Mary. She was the first-born in the order of grace, and was more beloved by God than any other saint. Eminent in gifts of grace were the patriarchs, the prophets, the apostles, the martyrs, the confessors, and the virgins; but Mary was adorned with more abundant grace than they. St. Bonaventure calls the grace which Mary received immense, because she was full of grace; and she contained in her bosom him whom the heavens and earth could not contain. The prudent giver, says Albertus Magnus, varies his gifts according to the end which he has in view in bestowing them; the greater the end, the greater the gift. But grace was given to Mary to prepare her to be the mother of God; to the other saints, to enable them to be his servants; immeasurably greater, therefore, was the gift bestowed upon Mary than that bestowed upon all the other saints. The gift which contains all other gifts is charity. Mary, therefore, was more beloved than every saint. She was the first-born also in the order of glory; for, when she was taken up into heaven, she was enthroned as queen of heaven and earth, and queen of all saints.

Her dignity as mother of God is the second motive of devotion to the blessed virgin. Her dignity is so great, says St. Thomas, that God himself cannot render it greater. This most august title of Mother of God, says the devout and learned Segneri, is an abyss of perfection ; and from this abyss, as from a constant and exhaustless source, well up in the Virgin the honors, almost without end, which she rightfully challenges. As all the extraordinary honors paid to Christ are owed to him because he is the only-begotten of the Father, so all the honors due to Mary flow from her being the mother of God made man. From Mary alone the Lord took flesh, and Mary alone can bear the title of Mother of God. Mary is, therefore, exalted in dignity far above all other creatures. A plant, says Albertus Magnus, is esteemed according to the fruit which it produces ; the fruit gives value and dignity to the plant ; no fruit can be found on earth or in heaven more sublime in dignity than that which Mary bore; amongst mere creatures, therefore, no loftier dignity is possible than that of Mary, mother of God. To declare of Mary, says St. Anselm, that she is mother of God, exceeds all exaltation that can be conceived beneath God himself.

The favors which we receive through Mary form the third motive for loving her. All the favors imparted to us through Mary, are found expressed in abridgment in the words of the evangelist: Mary, of whom was born Jesus, who is called Christ (*Matt.* i. 16). The world had been involved for four thousand years in the darkness of sin, and Mary caused the light of God to send forth its splendor over the earth. I, that is Mary, made that in the heavens there should rise light that never faileth (*Eccl.* xxiv. 6). The angels were awaiting the Savior of man, that the loss which the heavenly host had sustained in the rebellion of Lucifer might be repaired. Our first parents by their sin had closed the gates of Paradise and opened those of the abyss; and the souls of the departed just were sighing in expectation of the Messias. Mary gave birth to him who was made man to suffer for our salvation and deliver us by his death from the slavery of Satan under which we were groaning. Hence, in the doctrine of the Fathers, for these reasons she may be said to have co-operated in our redemption; because by her assiduous and humble prayers she hastened the Incarnation of the Word; because she gave her free consent to the Incarnation, and furnished human flesh to the only-begotten of the Most High; because she consented to the sacrifice on Calvary, and offered it up in heart in union with Jesus, her son. Through thee, says St. Cyril of Alexandria, through thee, O Mary, the only-begotten Son of God shone with true light to mortals sitting in darkness and in the shadow of death.

The love which Mary bears us, is the fourth motive which should cause us to honor her with unshaken affection. To feel convinced that she loves us with sincere motherly love, it is sufficient to reflect that, in the person of John, she was given to us as a mother by the dying Savior whilst she was standing at the foot of his cross. Woman, behold thy Son ! The love of a mother is a love implanted in her heart by nature. Can a woman forget her infant, asks the prophet Isaias, so as not to have pity on the son of her womb? (xlix.16). A spiritual bond is also stronger than a natural bond. Mary, therefore, having adopted us as her spiritual children, guards us with greater solicitude than a mother by nature guards her child. The graces which God bestows upon us are all bestowed in order to our spiritual life ; all Mary's exertions, therefore, in our behalf, aim at our spiritual welfare. For this reason the words of Ecclesiasticus are applied to her: I am the mother of fair love (*Eccl.* xxiv. 24). By nature she is the mother of Christ, by grace the mother of Christians. Her solicitude in behalf of her children is mystically foreshown in Queen Esther, who appeased by her prayers King Assuerus, and delivered from death the Jewish people, a figure of the Christian.

II.

Having considered the motives which urge us to love Mary with perseverance, let us now consider in what manner, principally, we should show our love. The fruit of devotion to the Virgin must be the destruction of sin. This is all the fruit, says the Lord speaking by Isaias, *that the sin thereof(of the house of Jacob) be taken away (Is.* xxvii. 9). The design of all the works of nature, of all the works of grace, of all the blessings, both temporal and spiritual, which God grants to us, either immediately by himself,— as in the Sacraments,—or mediately by the hands of his most holy mother,—the design of all these, is, says the devout Segneri, to destroy sin, and render us capable of the friendship of God and the eternal happiness which he holds prepared for those who are dear to him. If Mary yielded her consent to the Incarnation of the Word; if she was willing that her Son should offer himself to the Father as a victim of propitiation for our sins; if she accepted us as her children,—it was that sin might be banished from the world, the sinner reconciled with God, and restored to his rights as a child by grace of the Almighty and heir to the kingdom of heaven. She speaks to our hearts every day in the sentiments of the Redeemer: If you wish to enter into the joys of eternal life avoid sin and keep the commandments. Flee from sin as you would flee from the face of a serpent; its very aspect may infect you with poison and destroy your life.

We should love Mary from the heart. The first commandment of God is to love him with the whole heart. We cannot therefore love Mary more truly than by directing to her our thoughts and the affections of our soul. St. Bonaventure exclaims: O Mary, the sole memory of thee softens the feelings of my heart; thy loveliness consoles my spirit. Holy mother, thou who carriest away hearts by thy amiableness, hast thou not carried mine away?

Mary is our mother; we should therefore invoke her, reverence her, and honor her; we tribute the highest honor to her when we call upon her as our mother; as our teacher in the way of heaven; as our advocate, who obtains for us from her Son the forgiveness of our sins; as our spiritual and temporal benefactress. We also honor Mary by paying respect to her images, visiting her churches, reciting her Office or Holy Rosary. But what is most agreeable to her is the imitation of her virtues. To prove by our conduct that the sentiments of our hearts are in union with those of her own is the surest way to gain her protection. It would be but the merest adulation to pretend to reverence Mary, and call upon her aid, without imitating her examples. Beware, O Christian, says a devout servant of Mary, that Mary do not repent of having conceived thee, as did Rebecca, when she said: If it were to be so with me, what need was there to conceive? (*Gen.* xxv. 22). If Mary should have to grieve in this manner concerning any one of us, it were better for him that he had never been conceived.

ASPIRATION.

Jesus and Mary, I offer to you my heart and soul.

PRACTICE.

Resolve to be a dutiful child of Mary's and offer up to her all your devotions and all your works of piety that she may present them to her divine Son.

LITANY.

Read the Imitation of Christ.

SUNDAY.

*Prayer to the most Blessed Virgin Mary,
to obtain the Forgiveness of our Sins.*

Behold, O Mother of God, at thy feet a miserable sinner, who has recourse to thee and trusts in thee. I do not deserve that thou shouldst even look at me; but I know that thou, having seen thy Son die for the salvation of sinners, hast the greatest desire to help them. I hear all call thee the refuge of sinners, the hope of those who are in despair, and the help of the abandoned. Thou art, then, my refuge, my hope, and my help. Thou hast to save me by thy intercession. Help me, for the love of Jesus Christ; extend thy hand to a miserable creature who has fallen, and recommends himself to thee. I know that thy pleasure is to help a sinner to thy utmost; help me, therefore, now that thou canst do so. By my sins I have lost divine grace, and with it my soul; I now place myself in thy hands. Tell me what I must do to recover the favor of my Lord, and I will immediately do it. He sends me to thee that thou mayest help me, and 'He wills that I should have recourse to thy mercy, that not only the merits of thy Son, but also that thy intercession may help me to save my soul. To thee, then, I have recourse; do thou, who prayest for so many others, pray also to Jesus for me Ask Him to pardon me, and He will forgive me; tell Him that thou desirest my salvation, and he will save me; show how thou canst enrich those who trust in thee. Amen. Thus I hope, thus may it be.

MONDAY.

Prayer to the most Blessed Virgin Mary, to obtain holy Perseverance.

O Queen of Heaven, I now dedicate myself to thee, to be thy servant for ever; I offer myself to honor thee, and serve thee during my whole life; do thou accept me, and refuse me not, as I deserve. O my mother, in thee have I placed my hopes, through thy intercession do I expect every grace. I bless and thank God, who in His mercy has given me this confidence in thee, which I consider a pledge of my salvation. Alas! I have hitherto fallen, because I have not had recourse to thee. I now hope that, through the merits of Jesus Christ and thy prayers, I have obtained pardon. But I may again lose Divine grace; the danger is not past. My enemies do not sleep. How many new temptations have I still to conquer! Ah, my dear Mother, protect me, and permit me not again to fall; help me at all times. I know that thou wilt help me, and that with thy help I shall conquer. I fear that in time of danger I may neglect to call upon thee, and thus be lost. I ask thee, then, for this grace: obtain that, in the assaults of hell, I may always have recourse to thee, saying, Mary, help me. My Mother, permit me not to lose my God.

TUESDAY.

Prayer to the Blessed Virgin Mary, to obtain a good Death.

O Mary, my Mother, how shall I die? Even now that I think of my sins, and of that decisive moment on which my salvation or eternal damnation depends, of that moment in which I must expire and be judged, I tremble and am confounded. O my most sweet Mother, my hopes are in the blood of Jesus Christ and in thy intercession. O comfortress of the afflicted, do not, then, abandon me, cease not to console me in that moment of so great affliction. If I am now so tormented by remorse for sins committed, the uncertainty of pardon, the danger of relapse, and the rigor of Divine Justice, what will become of me then? Unless thou helpest me, I shall be lost. Before death obtain me great sorrow for my sins, thorough amendment, and fidelity to God during the remainder of my life. And when my last moment arrives, O Mary, my hope, help me in the great distress in which I shall then be; encourage me, that I may not despair at the sight of my sins, which the devil will place before me. Obtain that I may then invoke thee more frequently; so that I may expire with thy most sweet name and that of thy beloved Son on my lips. Nay, more, my Mother, but forgive my boldness, before I expire do thou come thyself and comfort me with thy presence. Thou hast granted this favor to so many of thy devout servants, I also desire and hope for it. I am a sinner, it is true; I do not deserve so great a favor; but I am thy servant. I love thee and have full confidence in thee. O Mary, I shall expect thee; do not deprive me of this consolation. At least, if I am not worthy of so great a favor, do thou help me from heaven, that I may leave this life loving God and thee, to love thee eternally in Paradise.

WEDNESDAY.

Prayer to the most Blessed Virgin Mary, to obtain Deliverance from Hell.

Beloved Mother, I thank thee for having saved me from hell as many times as I have deserved it by my sins. I was once condemned to that prison, and perhaps already, after the first sin, the sentence would have been put into execution, if thou, in thy compassion, hadst not helped me. Without even being asked by me, and only in thy goodness, thou didst restrain Divine Justice; and then, conquering my obduracy, thou didst draw me to have confidence in thee. O, into how many other sins should I have afterwards fallen, in the dangers in which I have been, hadst not thou, my loving Mother, preserved me by the graces which thou didst obtain for me! Ah, my Queen, continue to guard me from hell; for what will thy mercy, and the favors which thou hast shown me, avail me if I am lost? If I did not always love thee, now at least —after God—I love thee above all things· Never allow me to turn my back on thee and on God,who, by thy means has grant. ed me so many graces. My most amiable Mother, never allow me to have the misfortune to hate thee and curse thee for all eternity in hell.   Wilt thou endure to see a child of thine, who loves thee, lost? I shall be lost if I abandon thee.   But how can I ever forget the love thou hast borne me?   My Mother, since thou hast done so much to save me, complete the work, con‑ tinue the aid. If at a time when I lived forgetful of thee thou didst favor me so much, how much more may I not hope for now that I love thee and recommend my‑ self to thee!   No, he can never be lost who recommends himself to thee; he alone is lost who has not recourse to thee. Leave me not in my own hands, for I should then be lost; grant that I may always have recourse to thee.   Save me, my hope, save me from hell; but, in the first place, save me from sin, which alone can condemn me to it.

THURSDAY.

Prayer to the most Blessed Virgin Mary, to obtain Heaven.

O Queen of Paradise who reignest above all the choirs of angels, and who art the nearest of all creatures to God, I salute thee from this valley of tears, and beseech thee to turn thy compassionate eyes towards me. See, O Mary, in how many dangers I now am, and shall be as long as I live in this world, of losing my soul, of losing heaven and God. Ah, when will be that happy day on which I shall see myself safe at thy feet, and contemplate my Mother, who has done so much for my salvation? When shall I kiss that hand which has delivered me so many times from hell, and has dispensed me so many graces, when, on account of my sins, I deserved to be hated and abandoned by all? My Lady, in life I have been very ungrateful to thee; but if I get to heaven, I shall no longer be ungrateful: there I shall love thee as much as I can in every moment for all eternity, and shall make amends for my ingratitude by blessing and thanking thee for ever. I thank God with my whole heart, who gives me firm confidence in the blood of Jesus Christ and in thee, and in the conviction that thou wilt save me; that thou wilt deliver me from my sins; that thou wilt give me light and strength to execute the Divine Will; and, in fine, that thou wilt lead me to the gate of Paradise. Thy servants have hoped for all this, and not one of them was deceived. Beseech thy Son Jesus, as I also beseech Him, by the merits of His Passion, to preserve and always increase this confidence in me, and I shall be saved.

FRIDAY.

Prayer to the most Blessed Virgin Mary, to obtain Love towards her and Jesus Christ.

O Mary, I already know that thou art the most noble, the most pure, the most beautiful, the most benign, the most holy--in a word, the most amiable of all creatures. O that all knew thee, my Lady, and loved thee as thou dost merit! But I am consoled when I remember that in heaven and on earth there are so many happy souls who live enamoured of thy goodness and beauty. Above all, I rejoice that God Himself loves thee alone more than He loves all men and angels together. My most amiable Queen, I, a miserable sinner, love thee also; but I love thee too little· I desire a greater and more tender love towards thee; and this thou must obtain for me,since to love thee is a great mark of predestination, and a grace which God only grants to those whom He will save.

I see also,my Mother,that I am indeed under great obligations to thy Son. I see that He merits infinite love. Thou,who desirest nothing else but to see Him loved, hast to obtain me this grace above all others; obtain me great love for Jesus Christ. Thou obtainest all that thou willest from God; ah, then, be graciously pleased to obtain me the grace to be so united to the Divine Will that I may never more be separated from it. I do not ask of thee earthly goods, honors, or riches. I ask thee for that which thy heart desires most for me. I wish to love my God. Is it possible that thou refusest to second this, my desire, which is so pleasing to thee? Ah no, thou already helpest me; already thou prayest for me. Pray, pray, and cease not to pray until thou seest me safe in heaven, beyond the possibility of ever more losing my Lord, and certain to love Him for ever, together with thee, my dearest Mother.

SATURDAY.

Most holy Virgin Mary, Mother of God, I., N., although most unworthy to be thy servant, yet moved by thy wonderful compassion, and by my desire to serve thee, now choose thee, in presence of my guardian angel and of the whole celestial court, for my especial Patroness and Advocate, and I firmly purpose always to love and serve thee for the future, and to do whatever I can to induce others to love and serve thee also. I beseech thee, O Mother of God, and my most compassionate and loving Mother, by the blood which thy Son shed for me, to receive me into the number of thy servants, to be thy child and servant for ever. Assist me in all my thoughts, words, and actions, in every moment of my life, so that every step that I take, and every breath that I draw, may be directed to the greater glory of my God, and through thy most powerful intercession, may I never more offend my beloved Jesus, but may I glorify Him, and love Him in this life, and love thee, my most beloved and dear Mother, and thus love thee and enjoy thee in heaven for all eternity. Amen.

My Mother Mary, I recommend my

soul to thee, and especially at the hour of my death.

Prayer of Saint Thomas Aquinas.

O most blessed and most sweet Virgin Mary, full of mercy, to thy compassion I recommend my soul and body, my thoughts, actions, life, and death. O my Lady, help and strengthen me against the snares of the devil; obtain me true and perfect love, with which to love thy most beloved Son and my Lord Jesus Christ with my whole heart, and after Him to love thee above all things. My Queen and Mother, by thy most powerful intercession, grant that I may persevere in this love until death, and after death be conducted by thee to the kingdom of the blessed.

LITANY OF THE BLESSED VIRGIN.

Lord, have mercy on us.
Christ, have mercy on us.
Lord, have mercy on us.
Christ, hear us.
Christ, graciously hear us.
God, the Father of heaven, *have mercy on us.*

God, the Son, Redeemer of the world, *have mercy on us.*

God, the Holy Ghost, *have mercy on us.*

Holy Trinity, one God, *have mercy on us.*

Holy Mary,
Holy Mother of God,
Holy Virgin of virgins,
Mother of Christ,
Mother of divine grace,
Mother most pure,
Mother most chaste,
Mother undefiled,
Mother inviolate,
Mother most amiable,
Mother most admirable,
Mother of our Creator,
Mother of our Redeemer,
Virgin most prudent,
Virgin most venerable,
Virgin most renowned,
Virgin most powerful,
Virgin most merciful,
Virgin most faithful,
Mirror of justice,
Seat of wisdom,
Cause of our joy,
Spiritual vessel,
Vessel of honor,
Vessel of singular devotion,
Mystical rose,

Pray for us.

Tower of David,
Tower of ivory,
House of gold,
Ark of the covenant,
Gate of heaven,
Morning star,
Health of the weak,
Refuge of sinners,
Comfortress of the afflicted,
Help of Christians,
Queen of angels,
Queen of patriarchs,
Queen of prophets,
Queen of apostles,
Queen of martyrs,
Queen of confessors,
Queen of virgins,
Queen of all saints,
Queen conceived without original sin,
Queen of the most holy Rosary,

Pray for us.

Lamb of God, who takest away the sins of the world—*Spare us, O Lord!*

Lamb of God, who takest away the sins of the world—*Graciously hear us, O Lord!*

Lamb of God, who takest away the sins of the world—*Have mercy on us, O Lord.*

V. Pray for us, O holy Mother of God.

R. That we may be made worthy of the promises of Christ.

Let us pray.

Pour forth, we beseech Thee, O Lord, Thy grace into our hearts, that we, to whom the Incarnation of Christ Thy Son was made known by the message of an angel, may, by His passion and cross, be brought to the glory of His resurrection, through the same Christ our Lord. Amen.

———

LITANY OF OUR BLESSED LADY OF VICTORY.

Lord, have mercy on us.
Christ, have mercy on us. •
Lord, have mercy on us.
Christ, hear us.
Christ, graciously hear us.
God, the Father of heaven, *have mercy on us.*
God, the Son, Redeemer of the world, *have mercy on us.*
God, the Holy Ghost, *have mercy on us.*
Holy Trinity, one God, *have mercy on us.*
Our Lady of Victory,
Our Lady of Victory, triumphant Daughter of the Father,
Our Lady of Victory, triumphant Mother of the Son,
Our Lady of Victory, triumphant Spouse of the Holy Ghost,

Pray for us.

Our Lady of Victory, triumphant choice of the Most Holy Trinity,

Our Lady of Victory, triumphant in thy Immaculate Conception,

Our Lady of Victory, triumphant in crushing the head of the serpent,

Our Lady of Victory, triumphant over all the children of Adam,

Our Lady of Victory, triumphant over all our enemies,

Our Lady of Victory, triumphant in the embassy of the Angel Gabriel,

Our Lady of Victory, triumphant in thy espousal with St. Joseph,

Our Lady of Victory, triumphant at the scene of Bethlehem,

Our Lady of Victory, triumphant in thy flight into Egypt,

Our Lady of Victory, triumphant in thy exile,

Our Lady of Victory, triumphant in thy humble dwelling at Nazareth,

Our Lady of Victory, triumphant in finding thy Divine Child in the temple,

Our Lady of Victory, triumphant in the earthly life of Our Lord,

Our Lady of Victory, triumphant in His Passion and Death,

Our Lady of Victory, triumphant in the Resurrection,

Our Lady of Victory, triumphant in the Ascension,

Pray for us.

Our Lady of Victory, triumphant in the
descent of the Holy Ghost,

Our Lady of Victory, triumphant in thy sorrows,

Our Lady of Victory, triumphant in thy joys,

Our Lady of Victory, triumphant in thy entrance into the heavenly Jerusalem,

Our Lady of Victory, triumphant in the
angels who remained faithful,

Our Lady of Victory, triumphant in the felicity of the blessed,

Our Lady of Victory, triumphant in the
graces of the just,

Our Lady of Victory, triumphant in the an-
nouncement of the prophets,

Our Lady of Victory, triumphant in the desires of the patriarchs,

Our Lady of Victory, triumphant in the zeal
of the apostles,

Our Lady of Victory, triumphant in the light
of the evangelists,

Our Lady of Victory, triumphant in the wisdom of the doctors,

Our Lady of Victory, triumphant in the
crowns of the confessors,

Our Lady of Victory, triumphant in the
purity of the numerous bands of virgins,

Our Lady of Victory, triumphant in the triumphs of the martyrs,

Our Lady of Victory, triumphant in thy all-
powerful intercession,

Pray for us.

Our Lady of Victory, triumphant under thy
   many titles,
Our Lady of Victory, triumphant at the hour
   of our death,

Lamb of God, who takest away the sins of the
   world, *Spare us, O Lord.*
Lamb of God, who takest away the sins of the
   world, *Graciously hear us, O Lord,*
Lamb of God, who takest away the sins of the
   world, *Have mercy on us.*

V. Pray for us, O Blessed Lady of Victory !
R. That we may be made worthy of the promises
   of Christ.

Let us pray.

O Victorious Lady ! thou who hast ever such
powerful influence with thy Divine Son in conquering the hardest of hearts, intercede for those
for whom we pray, that their hearts being softened
by the rays of Divine grace, they may return
to the unity of the true Fath, through Christ
our Lord. Amen.

SALVE REGINA.

Hail, holy Queen, Mother of mercy, our life,
our sweetness, and our hope.

To thee do we cry, poor banished children of
Eve. To thee do we send up our sighs, mourning and weeping in this valley of tears.

Turn, then, most gracious advocate, thine eyes
of mercy towards us,

And after this, our exile, show unto us the

blessed fruit of thy womb, Jesus.

O clement, O loving, O sweet Virgin Mary.

Pray for us O holy Mother of God :

That we may be made worthy of the promises of Christ.

MEMORARE.

Remember, O most gracious Virgin Mary, that never was it known that any one who fled to thy protection, implored thy help, and sought thy intercession, was left unaided. Inspired with this confidence, I fly unto thee, O Virgin of virgins, my Mother. To thee I come; before thee I stand, sinful and sorrowful. O Mother of the Word Incarnate! despise not my petitions but, in thy mercy, hear and answer me. Amen.

PRINTED BY BENZIGER BROTHERS, NEW YORK